D1093960

nobu
WEST

This edition first published in 2006 by
Alhambra Editions, Alhambra House,
27–31 Charing Cross Road, London WC2H 0LS

Editorial Director	Jane O'Shea
Creative Director	Helen Lewis
Editor and project manager	Lewis Esson
Art direction and design	Vanessa Courtier
Photography	Eiichi Takahashi
Food styling	Nobu Matsuhisa and
	Mark Edwards
Production	Ruth Deary

British Library Cataloguing-in-Publication Data
A catalogue record for this book is available from the British
Library.

ISBN-13: 978 184400 402 7
ISBN-10: 1 84400 402 3

Printed in China

nobu
WEST

Nobu Matsuhisa
Mark Edwards

photographs by Eiichi Takahashi

ALHAMBRA
EDITIONS

contents

Contents

cocktails

sauces

glossary, index

Introduction

These days, cooking styles are not limited to their location and/or ingredients. With the Nobu restaurants now totalling sixteen worldwide, each new restaurant explores a fresh range of local ingredients and, in turn, contributes new ideas to the others. It's like a recipe book that is always growing.

Nobu West, the third book in the series, explores even more fully the confluence of cultures and cuisines that is now 'Nobu Style' cuisine. Although the recipes in it are still quintessentially Japanese in style and technique, the ingredients are much more those found mostly in the West.

The recipes are a result of not only our exploration of ingredients found in Europe and the Americas, but of our application of various creative approaches borne of knowledge gained from the distinct cuisines in the different countries in which we operate, in order to make 'Nobu-Style' cuisine more accessible to a wider audience.

As well as drawing on more readily available ingredients, we have attempted greater simplicity in the approach to the recipes in order to make it easier for you the reader to recreate and capture these dishes in the same fresh and vibrant manner as they were created. We hope you enjoy – even have fun – discovering and cooking the 120 Nobu-style dishes that follow.

We would like to thank all our suppliers who contributed the ingredients for this book, as well as the staff at Nobu London and Nobu Berkeley Street, without whose efforts this book would not have been possible. Also, a big 'thank you' to photographer Eiichi Takahashi for his amazing talent of capturing the moment and the essence of Nobu cuisine.

Nobuyuki Matsuhisa
Mark Edwards

London, July 2006

Abalone and white peach shooters

This chilled soup is served as a 'shooter' in a tall sherry glass, like our very popular oyster and quail's egg shooters. Abalone meat can be quite tough when raw, but this soup actually has a very silky texture, as both the abalone and the mountain yam are finely grated.

The Japanese mountain yam, or *yama imo*, is also known as 'sticky yam', and this property does help bind the liquid and give the soup a bit of body. For the flavour, it is important that you use white peach.

serves 4

1/8 cucumber, diced
4 cherry tomatoes, diced
1 white peach, peeled, stoned and diced
2 raw fresh abalone, shelled and cleaned
4cm piece of mountain yam (yama imo, see page 253)

for the stock:
400ml Dashi (see page 17)
1/4 teaspoon sea salt
2 tablespoons sake
2 tablespoons light soy sauce

1   Make the stock by mixing all the ingredients together and chill.

2   When ready to serve, spoon into 4 chilled small sherry glasses equal amounts of the diced cucumber, tomatoes and white peach.

3   Grate the abalone into a bowl using the fine mesh of a cheese grater (it can also be chopped by hand, but it must be very fine).

4   Grate the yam into the bowl using the fine cheese grater again; this will cause it to become very slimy.

5   Mix enough of the stock with the grated abalone and the yam to create a loose soup and then pour into the glasses to serve.

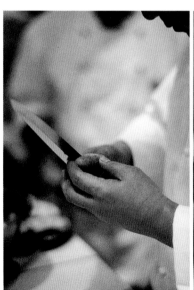

Chilled pea shoot soup with caviar

This soup makes a very refreshing way to start a meal, encapsulating the wonderful flavour of pea shoots when in season with a Japanese-flavoured soup base. The addition of caviar turns the soup into something quite special, and it should be served very cold and in small portions.

serves 4

150g pea shoots (see note, right; try to select the smallest
   shoots)
2 teaspoons light soy sauce
sea salt and freshly ground black pepper
crushed ice to serve
20g Golden Oscietra caviar

for the soup base (dashi)
5g konbu (dried seaweed, see page 251)
15g dried bonito flakes (see page 250)

1   First make the soup base (dashi): wipe the konbu with a damp cloth to remove any salt residue. In a non-reactive saucepan, heat 500ml of water and the konbu slowly over a medium heat.

2   Just before the water comes to the boil, take out the konbu and add the bonito flakes, then turn off the heat and leave to stand for 20–30 minutes.

3   Strain through a muslin-lined sieve.

4   In the rinsed-out pan, bring the dashi to a simmer, remove from the heat and add the pea shoots. Let stand for 5 minutes and then pour the pan contents into a blender and blend at high speed until smooth. (Be very careful to hold the lid down with a kitchen cloth as this mixture is hot, or wait until the soup is cold before blending.) Strain the soup through a fine strainer and refrigerate until very cold.

5   To serve, place 4 soup cups in a bowl of crushed ice to get them cold. Stir the soy sauce and salt and pepper to taste into the chilled soup, then pour the soup into the cups, leaving room for the caviar, and spoon the caviar equally on top of the soup.

note   Pea shoots, the young tender leaves and tendrils at the tips of the pea plant, have been used in the East for centuries, but are only now becoming readily available in the West.

Dublin bay prawn cocktail

This homage to the classic starter of the '60s is actually a quite simple but attractive dish that can be made with any type of large prawn, like tigers, or small langoustine. It is very light and makes a very healthy alternative to eating prawns or shrimps with mayonnaise or butter.

It is essential that you get the griddle, grill or salamander really very hot, so that the shellfish cook quickly, but for this reason you must make quite sure they don't get overcooked, or they become dry and tough, and this can happen in a matter of seconds.

serves 2

6 whole raw Dublin Bay prawns (see note, right)
vegetable oil for brushing
sea salt and freshly ground black pepper
Spicy lemon dressing (see page 242)
sprigs of shiso cress (see page 253) for garnish

1 Carefully peel the shell away from each raw Dublin Bay prawn, leaving just the tail fan.

2 Push a bamboo skewer through the whole length of each prawn, starting at the fan end (this will keep it straight during cooking).

3 Preheat a griddle pan, grill or salamander until good and hot. Brush the prawns with a little oil and season with salt and pepper.

4 Quickly cook the prawns on the griddle pan or under the salamander or grill for 2–3 minutes, taking care not to overcook them or they will toughen.

5 Arrange 3 of the skewers in a martini glass or similar, and drench with Spicy Lemon Dressing. Garnish each glass with a little of the shiso cress and serve.

note Dublin bay prawns are not actually prawns, but what the French call *langoustines* and the Italians *scampi*. They are, in fact, very small members of the lobster family and have delicious sweet flesh with a flavour that is like that of the very best lobster meat.

Nobu ceviche Greek style

This version of a traditional Greek salad is one that we make at our restaurant on the Greek island of Mykonos. The vegetables and feta cheese both go really well with our Ceviche Sauce and the salad is, of course, best served in summer. You can use any variety or colour of tomatoes that are available, as long as they are good and ripe.

serves 4

12 cooked Mediterranean prawns, peeled and deveined

3 plum tomatoes, cut into 2cm dice

150g feta cheese, cut into 2cm dice

2 teaspoons salt-packed capers, rinsed

1 tablespoon chopped coriander, plus some whole sprigs for garnish

1 small red onion, thinly sliced

1/4 cucumber, cut into 2cm dice

for the dressing

3 tablespoons Ceviche sauce (see page 247)

1 tablespoon extra-virgin olive oil

1 Put all the salad ingredients in a salad bowl.

2 Add the Ceviche sauce and the olive oil, and very gently mix together.

3 Garnish with a few sprigs of coriander and serve.

note Only dress the salad at the very last minute before serving it, or it will wilt the vegetables and cause the cheese to break up.

Fresh spring roll with lobster

These fresh spring rolls are simply a salad wrapped in rice paper. They should be made just before they are to be eaten. When working with the rice paper discs, try not to let them get too wet or they will become difficult to handle and tear easily.

serves 4

1 cooked lobster, about 400g–500g
8 rice paper discs, about 15cm in diameter
8 Chinese cabbage leaves, finely shredded
1/4 cucumber, finely diced

for the dressing
1 tablespoon Thai fish sauce (nam pla)
1 tablespoon water
2 tablespoons grapeseed oil
1 tablespoon fresh lemon juice
1 tablespoon chopped rinsed salt-packed capers, plus more whole capers to garnish
shichimi togarashi (see page 252)
freshly ground black pepper

1   Make the dressing by whisking the first five ingredients together and season with a pinch of shichimi togarashi and a generous twist of black pepper.

2   Remove the cooked lobster from its shell, rinse well, pat dry and cut into rough 3cm batons.

3   To assemble the spring rolls, lay a damp cloth on a flat work surface, then dip a circle of rice paper into warm water and place it on the damp cloth.

4   Place one-eighth of the shredded cabbage, lobster batons and cucumber dice in the middle of the rice paper.

5   Fold the bottom edge of the rice paper over the top of the filling and then roll it over to encase the filling. Fold in the right and then the left edges in towards the centre and finish by rolling it into a cylinder. Make 7 more rolls in the same way.

6   Serve the rolls garnished with some whole capers, if you like, with the dressing in a separate bowl. Dunk the rolls in the dressing to eat them.

note   To cook your own lobster, see page 59. When buying ready-cooked lobster, check that they are a bright red-orange colour, have a fresh aroma and that the tail section will spring back into a curled position after being straightened out. When shelling, all the lobster is edible, except for the small stomach (hard sac) behind the head and the dark intestinal vein running down the back of the tail, so remove and discard these.

Oysters with mint and cucumber salsa

The freshness of the mint in the salsa makes a surprisingly good foil for the oysters.

serves 2

6 fresh oysters
crushed ice, to serve

for the salsa
30g finely diced deseeded cucumber
30g finely chopped red onion
4 tablespoons Ponzu (see page 248)
1 tablespoon chopped fresh mint

1 Open the oysters (see page 40) and turn each one over in their curved half-shell. Arrange on a bed of crushed ice in a suitable serving dish.

2 Make the salsa by mixing all the ingredients together.

3 Spoon a little of the salsa over the top of each oyster and serve immediately

4 If you like, you can garnish the dish with some carrot and cucumber shavings for added colour, and one or two of the discarded top shells.

note When making the salsa, only add the mint once you are ready to serve the oysters, as it will go brown if left in the salsa for any time.

Scottish mussels with matsuhisa salsa

The salsa and the red chilli slices give the mussels a really spicy zing, making this a great dish to serve as finger food or as an appetizer. The shredded daikon makes an unusual and eye-catching alternative to the more usual crushed ice or sea salt as a base for the cooked mussels.

for the Matsuhisa salsa

60g finely chopped onion
1 tablespoon soy sauce
100ml rice vinegar
1 tablespoon grapeseed oil
1/2 teaspoon chilli oil
1/2 teaspoon sea salt
1/4 teaspoon chilli garlic sauce (see page 250)
1/4 teaspoon finely grated ginger
10g finely chopped parsley leaves

1   First make the Matsuhisa salsa: rinse the onion in cold water to remove the sharpness, then drain well. In a bowl, mix the drained onion with the rest of the ingredients except the parsley.

2   Wash the mussels under cold running water and check they are clean, removing any beards and discarding any mussels that stay open when tapped.

3   Place them in a steamer with a pinch of salt added to the water and steam for 5 minutes. Remove from the steamer and discard any mussels that haven't opened. Leave to cool a little.

4   Remove the top half of the shell of each mussel and loosen the mussel in the bottom shell with a teaspoon or knife.

serves 4

12–16 fresh live mussels
pinch of salt
shredded daikon (see page 250)
1/2 lime
1 long red chilli, cut across into thin slices

5   Arrange on a bed of shredded daikon in a suitable dish, set around a lime half. Stir the parsley into the salsa and spoon a little of it over each mussel. Top with a slice of red chilli.

note   When buying your mussels, allow 2 or 3 more than you need in case they are dead (they won't close when tapped or won't open when cooked).

Spanish mackerel sashimi with dried miso

The intense flavour of the dried miso takes the place of salt in this dish and adds a good deal of kick to the mackerel. Spanish mackerel is much larger than the common mackerel, rather more like the tuna, which is a relative of both. It has a very superior flavour. You could, of course, use either tuna or ordinary mackerel for this dish.

makes 5

150g fresh Spanish mackerel, filleted and skinned
1 teaspoon finely chopped garlic
1 teaspoon finely chopped ginger
1 teaspoon Dried miso (see page 249)
black pepper
5 chicory leaves
1/2 lime, peeled and peel reserved
finely shredded spring onion, for garnish

1   Using a large knife, chop the mackerel fillet into rough mince (do not chop so much that it turns into a paste) and place it in a bowl.

2   Add the garlic, ginger and half the dried miso, and season with a little black pepper, then very gently mix everything together.

3   Spoon the mackerel mixture into the centre of the chicory leaves and arrange them around the lime half on a serving dish. Sprinkle with the rest of the dried miso and place some of the shredded spring onion on the top of each leaf. Arrange the lime peel on the lime half to complete the garnish.

note   When eating, squeeze a little of the juice from the lime over the top. This dish can also be served as an appetizer or canapé.

Scottish beef tataki

The tataki principle of quickly searing the beef on the outside in a very hot pan gives a wonderful texture, taste and colour contrast between the raw centre and the seared outside. The well-browned and caramelized exterior of the beef also develops more flavour in the rest of the beef by imbuing it with a gentle, sweet smokiness. For this sort of quick treatment where most of the beef remains raw, you do, of course, have to use the very best beef, which is why we choose Scottish beef for our beef tataki.

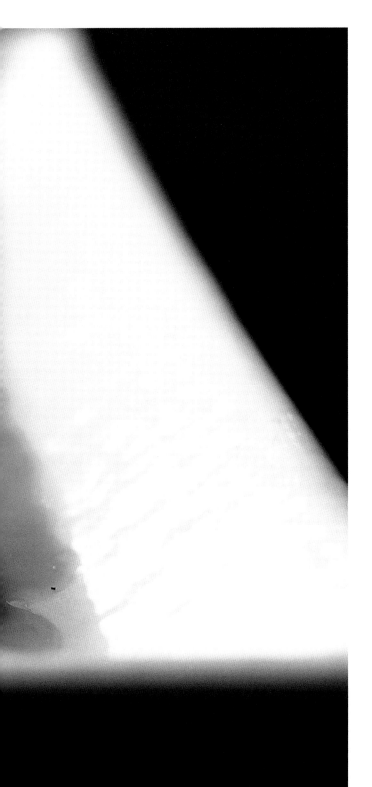

serves 4

ice cubes
200g fillet of beef, preferably Scottish
oil for frying
freshly ground black pepper
2 tablespoons thinly sliced spring onion
2–3 garlic cloves, thinly sliced

for the Tosa-zu sauce
5 tablespoons soy sauce
8 tablespoons rice vinegar
4g dried bonito flakes (see page 250)

1 First make the Tosa-zu sauce: warm the soy sauce and vinegar slightly in a small saucepan (taking care not to let the mixture boil) and add the dried bonito flakes. Leave to cool to room temperature and then strain out the bonito flakes.

2 Have ready a bowl of iced water. Season the beef fillet with black pepper and heat a dry non-stick frying pan until very hot, then sear each surface of the beef for 5 seconds, ensuring that all the outside has been completely seared and no red meat is visible. Then plunge the beef into the iced water to stop the cooking process. Remove, pat dry with kitchen paper and chill in the refrigerator.

3 Bring about 2cm of oil in a saucepan to 150°C and slowly deep-fry the garlic slices in it until they turn a light golden brown. Remove immediately and drain on kitchen paper.

4 Thinly slice the beef (about 2–3mm thick) and arrange the slices on a flat serving dish.

5 Top each slice of beef with a little of the spring onion and a slice of fried garlic. Spoon some of the sauce around the edges of the beef and serve.

Scallop chawan mushi

Chawan mushi is a very delicate, light stock-enriched egg custard. In Japan it is regarded by many as a soup, even though the egg sets in the steaming process. This dish can also be served cold in the summer; just refrigerate after cooking.

serves 4

3 medium eggs
500ml Dashi (see page 17)
2 tablespoons sake
2 tablespoons soy sauce
1/2 teaspoon sea salt
4 large raw fresh scallops cleaned, any coral removed
4 teaspoons caviar
fine strips of pared lime rind for garnish (optional)

1 In a bowl, whisk the eggs until smooth, then add the dashi, sake, soy sauce and salt. Mix well and strain the mixture through a very fine sieve or cheesecloth.

2 Slice each scallop across its depth to produce 3 or 4 rounds and arrange them overlapping on the bottom of a small bowl suitable for steaming.

3 Carefully pour the egg mixture into the each of the bowls and remove any bubbles that have formed on the surface with the edge of some kitchen paper.

4 Cover the bowls with clingfilm and very gently steam them for 15–20 minutes, until the egg mixture has set. The chawan mushi is done when a cocktail stick inserted into the centre comes out clean.

5 Remove the clingfilm and place a teaspoon of caviar on each dish. Garnish with some strips of pared lime rind if you like. Serve with a spoon.

note Try to buy diver scallops if you can find them, as not only are they usually larger, but they are generally in better condition and they are much more ecologically sound.

Cornish crab harumaki

Harumaki are a Japanese version of the spring roll. This really delicious combination of tasty fresh Cornish crab meat with shiitake mushrooms and shiso leaves encased in a crispy skin and served with a tangy dipping sauce continues to be a favourite in all the restaurants.

serves 4

4 shiitake mushrooms
4 shiso leaves (see page 253), plus more to garnish
4 spring roll wrappers
200g cooked crab (preferably Cornish) claw meat
salt and freshly ground black pepper
flour for sealing
oil for deep-frying

for the Spicy ponzu dip
150ml Ponzu (see page 248)
2 teaspoons green Tabasco sauce
juice of 1 lime
1 tablespoon finely chopped ginger
1 tablespoon finely chopped red onion
2 teaspoons finely chopped deseeded red chilli
1/2 tablespoon finely chopped fresh coriander

1   First make the dip by combining all the ingredients together well and pour into a small dipping bowl.

2   Cut the mushrooms into 5mm slices and halve the shiso leaves.

3   Working with one spring roll wrapper at a time, cut each sheet diagonally in half and place on a flat surface with the point of its triangle shape facing away from you.

4   Place a shiso leaf half in the centre of each triangle, then 25g of crab meat on top of that and finish with 2 slices of shiitake mushroom lengthways on top of the crab. Season with a little salt and freshly ground black pepper.

5   Fold the left side of the wrapper in over the filling towards the centre, followed by the right side. Roll the wrapper up away from you and seal the end with a little flour and water mixture. Care should be taken that the roll is completely sealed at the edges, otherwise the oil will get inside the roll while it is frying.

6   When all the harumaki are made, heat oil for deep-frying to a temperature of 180°C and fry the rolls in the hot oil until golden brown all over. Drain briefly on kitchen paper and serve as soon as possible, with the bowl of Spicy ponzu dip and garnished with more shiso leaves.

note   Any type of spring roll wrappers or wonton skins will do . Confusingly, imported genuine Japanese ones will often be sold as 'egg roll' wrappers, which is what they are called in the USA.

Matsuhisa prawns London-style

These prawns are designed to be eaten in one go, in order to experience the full effect of all of the flavours together – the sweetness of the prawns, the citrus tang of the yuzu and the saltiness of the caviar. It is very popular as a canapé.

serves 2

5 raw tiger prawns in the shell, each around 30g
1 tablespoon clarified butter (see page 126)
1 cep (porcini) mushroom, cut into 5
3 shiso leaves, cut in half lengthwise
2 teaspoons Creamy spicy sauce (see page 246)
5 teaspoons Oscietra caviar
2 teaspoons yuzu juice (see page 253)

1   To prepare the raw prawns, first remove the heads, then peel the shell, leaving the tail piece intact. Cut along the back and remove the black intestinal tract or 'vein', then rinse under cold water and drain.

2   Make an cut along the middle of the back, but not all the way through, to butterfly each prawn, and lightly score lines at 45 degrees across the prawn with the heel of the knife blade to prevent the prawn from curling up too much during cooking.

3   Heat the clarified butter in a frying pan and sauté the mushrooms until just cooked.

4   Preheat the oven to 150°C/gas 2. On the cut side of each prawn, place a piece of shiso leaf, a piece of cep and a little of the Creamy spicy sauce. Fold the end of the prawn over towards the tail and secure with a cocktail stick.

5   Bake in the oven for 3–4 minutes, or until the prawns are just cooked through and opaque. Transfer to a serving dish and top each prawn with a teaspoon of caviar and a little of the yuzu juice.

Oysters with pancetta

This baked oyster dish is very simple and quick to make, but it is important to ensure that the pancetta is sliced very thinly, so the oysters will cook quickly.

serves 4

12 rock oysters
200g salt
white of 1 egg
6 thin slices of pancetta (see above)
1/2 lime to serve
flat parsley leaves to garnish

1   Remove the oysters from their shells (see note, below) and rinse with cold water, then drain well.

2   Wash the bottom (curved) halves of the shells to remove any sand or shell debris and wipe dry with kitchen paper.

3   Preheat the oven to 180°C/gas 4. Mix the salt with the egg white to use as a base for the shells to bake on. Arrange 12 little piles on an ovenproof dish around the lime half, then place a cleaned shell on top of each mound.

4   Cut the pancetta slices in half and wrap each oyster in a piece. Place each on a prepared shell.

5   Bake in the oven for 3–4 minutes and serve while still hot, each shell garnished with a parsley leaf.

note   To open an oyster, place your thumb about a centimetre from the end of the oyster knife to prevent it from sliding along the oyster shell, and insert the blade in between the two valves at one side of the muscle 'hinge' at the back of the shell. Wedge the knife into the 'hinge' to cut through the muscle from the side. Lift or twist the knife to open the shell.

Whelks 'escargot style'

This is an adaptation of the classic French *escargots à la bourguignonne*, but using sea snails – which is what whelks are. Only the small amount of soy sauce and the pinch of shichimi togarashi that differentiate the garlic and shallot butter used to stuff the creatures.

serves 4

8 large live whelks

for the garlic and parsley butter
200g butter
4 garlic cloves, finely chopped
50g flat-leaf parsley, finely chopped
50g shallot, finely chopped
2 teaspoons soy sauce
juice of 1 lemon
sea salt and freshly ground black pepper
pinch of shichimi togarashi (see page 252)

to serve
sea salt
egg white

1   To make the garlic and parsley butter, allow the butter to soften at room temperature and mix in the rest of the ingredients.

2   Scrub the whelks with a scourer under cold running water. Place in a large pan of salted boiling water and cook for 5 minutes, then drain and allow to cool.

3   Remove the whelk meat from the shell with a skewer (turning the shell while doing this makes it easier to extract all of the meat). Cut away the guts and discard. Rinse the meat and the shells to remove any sand, then chop the meat into large pieces, place back in the shells and pack with the butter mixture.

4   Preheat the oven to 200°C/gas 6 and crumple some foil on a baking sheet (this will helps prevent the shells falling over). Place the shells carefully on to it, so that when the butter melts it will remain in the shell, and bake for 10–12 minutes until the butter is bubbling.

5   Serve on a bed of salt mixed with a little egg white (see page 44), which will keep them upright.

note   Although whelks are available all year round, they are at their best in the summer months.

Scallops with spicy black bean sauce

The scallops are baked in their cleaned curved shells with some shredded cabbage and leek, and pieces of oyster mushroom, all tossed in Spicy black bean sauce, which produces a very tasty sauce in the bottom of the shell.

serves 2

2 large fresh live scallops
30g cabbage, thinly shredded
30g leek, thinly shredded
30g oyster mushrooms, cut into 2cm pieces
4 tablespoons Spicy black bean sauce (see page 246)
5g dried wakame seaweed, reconstituted
freshly ground black pepper

to serve
sea salt
egg white

1   Preheat the oven to 200°C/gas 6. Scrub the outside of the scallop shells. Then, using a knife, open the scallop shells and extract the scallop meat. Remove the beard and the frilly outer membrane from each scallop muscle and discard. Scrub the inside of the deepest shell from each scallop and pat dry.

2   In a bowl, dress the cabbage, leek, oyster mushrooms and scallops with the Spicy black bean sauce. Divide the mixture between the bottoms of the deep scallop shells, placing the scallops in the centre. Season with pepper and top with the wakame.

3   Bake in the oven for 6–8 minutes, until the scallop is just cooked through.

4   Serve on a bed of salt mixed with a little egg white, which will keep them upright.

note   If you can't get fresh scallops in their shells, you can use any pre-shelled fresh scallop and cook them in an ovenproof earthenware dish.

Spicy quail tempura

In this recipe, the quail is first dipped in soy milk and then in seasoned flour, to give the outside a lovely crunchy texture. The quail can be eaten with the fingers, holding it by the bones.

serves 2

1 whole dressed quail
vegetable oil for deep-frying
1/2 lime
Red anticucho sauce (see page 246)

for the coating

75g flour
1/2 teaspoon cayenne pepper
2 teaspoons dried oregano
1 teaspoon ground cumin
1/2 teaspoon salt
1 teaspoon freshly ground black pepper
3 tablespoons soya milk

1 Remove the legs and the breasts of the quail from the carcass. Then remove the thigh bone from the legs, leaving the drumsticks. Clean the ends of the wing bones and drumsticks by scraping with a knife, which will ensure that they don't become too dark while frying.

2 Make the coating by mixing together all the ingredients except the soya milk.

3 Heat oil for deep-frying to 180°C. Dip the quail legs and breasts into the soya milk and then into the seasoned flour, making sure that they are well coated with the mixture.

4 Deep-fry the legs first for 30 seconds, then add the breasts and continue to fry both for a further 3 minutes, or until just cooked. Remove with a draining spoon and drain on kitchen paper.

5 Arrange on a serving dish accompanied by quarters of lime and a dipping cup of the Red anticucho sauce.

note Tempura items needn't always be cooked in batter, but can be coated in this simple way with seasoned flour. This treatment works equally well with other small birds, like pigeon.

Foie gras with mustard miso and pumpkin chips

Here the sweet flavour of the pumpkin and the mustard in the miso give another dimension to freshly sautéed foie gras.

serves 4

1 small butternut squash
vegetable oil for frying
200g fresh duck foie gras, at room temperature
sea salt and freshly ground black pepper
2 tablespoons Mustard miso (see page 247)
flat parsley leaves for garnish

1 Cut off the top cylindrical part of the squash and peel it, making sure all the outside skin is completely removed. Then slice the squash cylinder as thinly as possible into discs 1–2mm thick.

2 Bring a pan of oil 4cm deep to 150°C and fry the pumpkin rounds a few at a time, until golden and crisp, then drain on kitchen paper. Care should be taken when frying the pumpkin that the chips do not become too dark in colour.

3 Slice the foie gras into eight 25g pieces about 1cm thick. Season these with salt and pepper, and sauté in a very hot, dry frying pan for 1 minute on each side, then drain on kitchen paper.

4 To assemble, place a piece of foie gras on each pumpkin chip and drizzle a little Mustard miso over each one, then top with a parsley leaf. Serve on a flat dish, as soon as possible, as the pumpkin chips will become soft if left for too long.

note When frying foie gras, it must be done very fast in a very hot dry pan, otherwise it will just melt.

Pimientos de Padrón

Named after the town of Padrón in the Spanish province of Galicia, these wonderful small sweet green peppers are very much like their Japanese cousin the shishito pepper. About one in every twelve or so of these little fellows is actually hot and this makes it fun when eating to see who gets the heat. They can be either grilled or fried. Sprinkled with a little sea salt, they make an excellent start to a meal.

serves 2

12 pimientos de Padrón
sea salt

1   Preheat a hot grill, griddle pan or barbecue.

2   Place 6 peppers on 2 parallel bamboo skewers. Using 2 skewers in this way stops the peppers rotating on the skewer while cooking and thus helps them to cook evenly. Do the same with the other peppers.

3   Place the racks of peppers on the hot grill, griddle or barbecue and cook for 1–2 minutes until the skins begin to blister and the peppers have become slightly soft.

4   Sprinkle with sea salt and serve while still hot.

note   When using bamboo skewers on a barbecue, it is a good idea to soak them in water beforehand, to help prevent them charring over the heat.

salads

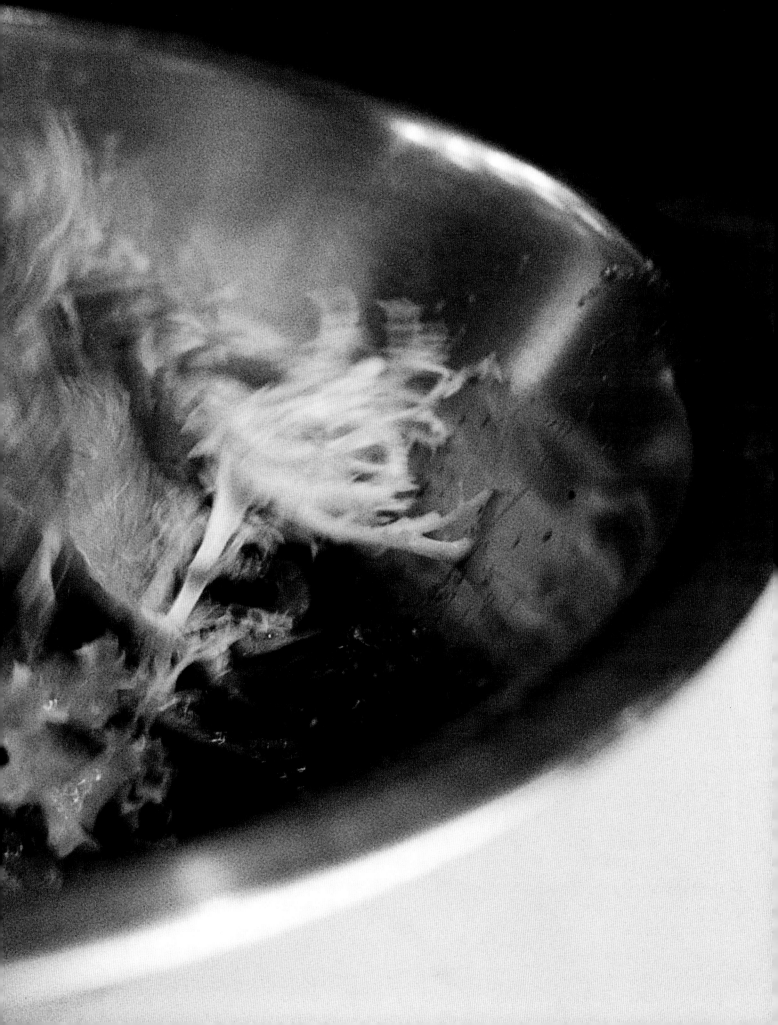

Turnip salad with scallops

This is very simple to prepare and makes a really attractive finished dish. The contrast between the textures of the crisp vegetables and the soft scallops makes for an interesting combination, which is then accentuated by the sharp citrus kick of the dressing.

serves 4

6 baby turnips
6 large radishes
4 large shelled scallops
¹/₂ lime
pinch of sea salt

for the Yuzu ponzu dressing
2 tablespoons Yuzu dressing (see page 63)
2 tablespoons Ponzu (see page 248)

1   To make the Yuzu ponzu dressing, combine the Yuzu dressing and Ponzu, and mix well.

2   Slice the turnips and radishes very thinly (about 1mm) lengthways on a mandolin and set aside.

3   Slice the scallops into thin discs, trying to get as many slices as you can from each scallop.

4   Arrange alternating slices of radish and turnip around the edge of a serving plate, making sure that each slice overlaps the previous one, and continue until the circle is complete.

5   Repeat the same process again, only this time make the circle smaller in the centre and alternate slices of scallop, radish and turnip, so the slices begin to resemble the petals of a flower.

6   Place the lime half in the centre, sprinkle the dish with sea salt and then carefully pour the sauce over the top of the salad.

notes   Try to find the smallest baby turnips you can, so the outside skin won't require peeling. A mandolin grater is essential for this dish, preferably a Japanese mandolin, in order to get the slices as thin as possible.

If you can, get radishes with some of their green stalks still attached and slice with some of these still on for an even more attractive presentation.

Crabmeat and punterella salad with spicy lemon and caper dressing

Punterella is a delicious salad green that is very popular in Italy. It has a rather bitter taste, resembling that of chicory (it is often called 'wild chicory'), which is actually quite addictive. In this very simple recipe, we combine white crab meat and a zesty lemon dressing to make a perfect accompaniment to the punterella.

serves 4

1 head of punterella
5 tablespoons Spicy lemon dressing (see page 242)
2 tablespoons chopped capers
200g cooked white crab meat

1 Rinse the punterella well and remove and discard the thick head and stalks, keeping the smaller tender pieces. Place these in a mixing bowl and dress with 3 tablespoons of the Spicy lemon dressing. Toss well to coat.

2 Arrange the dressed punterella on a serving dish, sprinkle the capers and crab meat on top and dress again with the remaining dressing.

note You can use any bitter salad leaf, such as chicory, frisée or radicchio, if punterella is not available.

Lobster and watercress salad with watercress dressing

The combination of fresh lobster and peppery watercress, together with the crunch of black sesame seeds, makes this a satisfying and very refreshing salad.

serves 4–6

1 live lobster (about 350g)
sea salt
iced water
bunches of watercress
2 teaspoons black sesame seeds
1/2 yellow pepper, deseeded and cut into fine strips

for the Watercress dressing
1 bunch of watercress
100ml rice vinegar
5 tablespoons grapeseed oil
2 teaspoons sea salt
1 teaspoon freshly milled black pepper

1 Put the lobster in the freezer for about 20 minutes, so it goes into a deep sleep and won't be aware of the next stage.

2 Bring a saucepan of salted water large enough to cover the lobster to the boil. Plunge the lobster head first into the water, bring back to the boil and simmer for 6 minutes. Remove the lobster and plunge it into a bowl of iced water to cool.

3 Remove the tail and claws from the body and crack the shell from meat. Cut the meat into bite-sized slices.

4 Make the salad: remove the thicker stems (which should be saved for the dressing) from the watercress, then roughly chop and place in a mixing bowl.

5 Make the dressing: pick all the leaves and smaller stems from the watercress and combine all the larger stems together with the reserved stems from the other bunch. Blanch the large stems in boiling salted water for 30 seconds and then refresh in iced water. Drain and chop together with the leaves and smaller stems. Add all the other dressing ingredients to a blender and blend together, adding the chopped blanched stems and leaves a little at a time until smooth.

6 Add a small amount of dressing to the watercress in the mixing bowl, sprinkle with a little of the black sesame seeds and mix gently.

7 Place the salad to one side of the centre of a serving dish and spoon the remaining dressing around the edge, then arrange the lobster pieces to the side of the salad.

8 Garnish the salad with the slices of yellow pepper and sprinkle everything with more black sesame seeds.

note The dressing should be made and used at the last minute, as the vinegar quickly turns the watercress brown.

Salmon tataki with paper-thin salad

Using paper-thin slices of baby vegetables instead of salad leaves gives this dish an interesting twist. The vegetables are first plunged into ice-cold water to give them a crunchy texture that contrasts nicely with the seared salmon sashimi.

serves 4

200g skinless boneless fresh salmon fillet
freshly ground black pepper
Jalapeño dressing (see page 242)

for the Paper-thin salad
2 baby carrots
2 baby green courgettes
2 baby yellow courgettes
2 baby turnips
4 red radishes
2 baby beetroots
bowlful of iced water

1   Preheat a non-stick frying pan until medium-hot and season the salmon fillets with black pepper, then sear them for 5 seconds on each side. Make sure that all the outside has been completely seared and has turned white. Immediately plunge them into iced water to stop the cooking process. Drain and pat dry with kitchen paper, then refrigerate.

2   Prepare the salad: keeping the beetroots to one side, slice the baby vegetables lengthways very thinly (about 1mm thick) on a mandolin grater into a bowl of iced water. Leave them in the iced water for 1 hour; this will cause them to tighten up and become crunchy. Repeat the same process with the beetroot, but place the slices in a separate bowl of water, to stop the colour running into the other vegetables, and rinse until the water becomes clear, then add some ice to chill. You my want to wear disposable gloves for this, to prevent staining your hands.

3   Drain the baby vegetables and the beetroots separately and then mix them together.

4   Pour some of the Jalapeño dressing on the bottom of a serving dish, so that it completely covers the base.

5   Cut the chilled seared salmon into slices about 5mm thick and arrange across the centre of the plate, then place the vegetable salad in the centre on top of the salmon.

Tomatillo and percebes salad

Percebes, also known as gooseneck barnacles, are almost prehistoric in appearance and grow in clumps on rocky shores all around the Atlantic. They are particularly revered in Spain and Portugal, where they are eaten quickly steamed or even raw. They have a slightly sweet flavour with an exquisitely strong taste of the sea, and here this is complemented by the gently acidic taste of the tomatillos. Also known as the Spanish tomato in Mexico, from where it originates, the tomatillo resembles a green tomato, so you can use these if you can't find any tomatillos.

serves 4

500g fresh percebes
sea salt
bowl of iced water
2 tomatillos
4 radishes

for the Yuzu dressing
50ml yuzu juice (see page 253)
25ml soy sauce
1/3 teaspoon freshly ground black pepper
1/2 teaspoon finely chopped garlic
6 tablespoons grapeseed oil

1   Blanch the percebes in boiling salted water for 1 minute, then refresh in iced water. When cold, peel them by pinching the outer tube just below the 'hoof-shaped' plates and prising it off with your fingernails. This will reveal the pinkish-white, fleshy tube-like neck inside, which can be pulled or cut off. This is the edible portion of the percebes. Discard the outer skin and hooves.

2   Make the Yuzu dressing by mixing all the ingredients together.

3   Slice the tomatillos and radishes thinly and arrange on a serving dish, alternating each slice to form a circle in the centre of the dish. Arrange the percebes in the middle and drench with about half the Yuzu dressing (keep the rest in the fridge for another seafood salad, like the Turnip salad with scallops on pages 54–55).

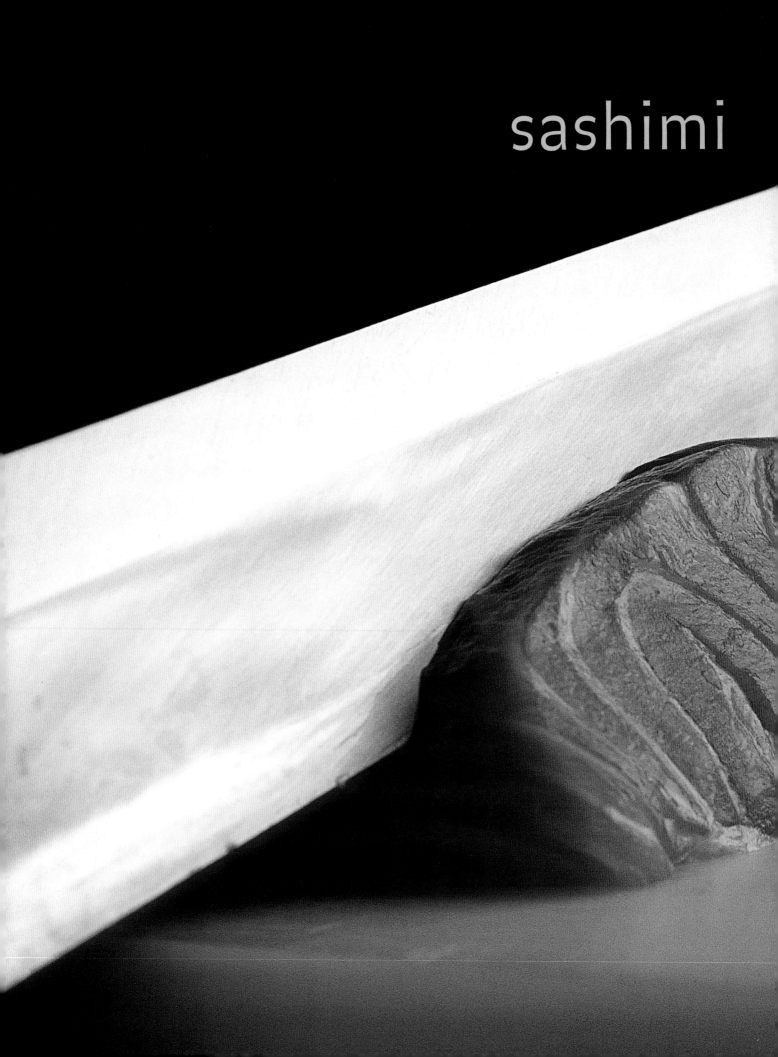

sashimi

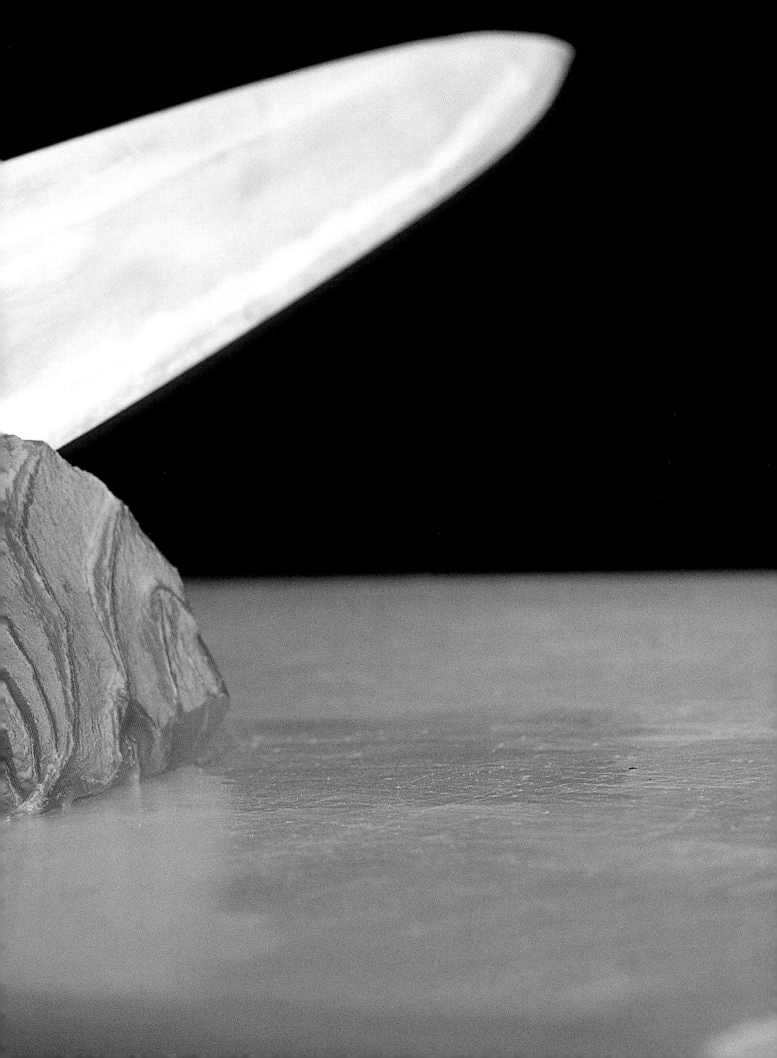

Lobster carpaccio

In this dish, the raw lobster is sliced very thinly and hot olive oil is poured over the top. This releases the delicate flavours of the lobster and the aromas of ginger and garlic.

serves 4

1 small live lobster, about 200–300g
1 tablespoon chopped chives
1/2 garlic clove, smashed to a paste with the flat of a knife
1 tablespoon finely shredded ginger
sea salt and freshly ground black pepper
1 tablespoon Yuzu dressing (see page 63)
small quantity of extra-virgin olive oil
few green olives, halved
few tatsoi leaves (see page 253)

1   Put the lobster in the freezer for about 20 minutes, so it goes into a deep sleep and won't be aware of the next stage.

2   Bring a saucepan of salted water large enough to cover the lobster to the boil. Plunge the lobster head first into the water for 30 seconds, remove and plunge into a bowl of iced water to cool. This will enable the meat to be easily removed from the shell.

3   Remove the tail and claws from the body and carefully crack the shells and gently remove the tail and claw meat. Slice the tail meat into medaillons about 5mm thick; cut the claw meat into 5mm thick slices and keep separate.

4   Lay a large piece of clingfilm on a chopping board and lay the tail medaillons on top of the cling film, allowing a little space in between each slice. Cover with another large piece of cling film.

5   With a meat mallet, gently bat out each tail piece as thinly as possible, about 1–2mm, taking care not to tear holes in the meat. Peel away the top layer of clingfilm by holding down on each flattened piece one at a time until the clingfilm is removed.

6   Place the lobster meat still attached to the bottom layer of clingfilm on the centre of the plate with the clingfilm uppermost. Gently peel away the clingfilm, again holding down each flattened piece of meat so that all the flattened lobster medaillons are left on the plate.

7   Dab the medallions with a little of the garlic purée and sprinkle the ginger and the chopped chives evenly on top. Season with a little sea salt and freshly ground black pepper, then drizzle the Yuzu dressing over the top.

8   Heat the olive oil a small pan it just begins to smoke and pour it over the lobster slices to sear the top. Garnish the middle with the sliced claws in the centre, some green olive halves on top of those and the tatsoi leaves.

Octopus carpaccio

This is a novel way to serve octopus and makes an attractive finished dish. The octopus is cooked and the tentacles are pressed together to form a sausage, which is then sliced and dressed with dried miso, olive oil and lemon juice.

serves 4

1 fresh Mediterranean or Atlantic octopus
1 teaspoon lemon juice
1 tablespoon olive oil
1/2 tablespoon chopped chives
1 teaspoon Dried miso (see page 249)

1   To prepare the octopus: pound the tentacles with the end of a piece of daikon or a wooden mallet to help tenderize the meat. Next cut a slit around the beak of the octopus (found in the middle of where the tentacles join the head) and remove the beak. Turn the head of the octopus inside out and remove all the innards and the eggs, if any. Rinse well under cold running water and remove any sinews in the head with a knife. Turn the head back out the right way and place in a ceramic mortar. Put your hand inside the head and rub the octopus around the bowl for 5–10 minutes, to help remove the sliminess (which appears like beaten egg white in the bowl) and any sand that is in the tentacles (salt can be added at this stage to speed the process up, but it will toughen the flesh). When all the slime has gone, rinse well under cold running water again, not forgetting inside the head.

2   Fill a saucepan with enough water to cover the octopus, salt it generously (30g salt to each litre of water), bring to the boil and slowly place the octopus in the water, tentacles first. Bring back to the boil, cover and reduce the heat to a gentle simmer, then simmer for 30–40 minutes, depending on the size of the octopus, until tender.

3   When cooked, remove the octopus from the water and cut off the 8 tentacles where they join the head – this should be done while it is still fairly hot. While the tentacles are still warm, spread a piece of clingfilm on a bamboo mat and lay the tentacles side by side, alternating the thick and thin ends on each side. The roll needs to be about 6cm in diameter (if the tentacles are very large and they are too big to roll up in the mat, make a second mat). Roll up the mat and tie tightly with string, then place in the freezer while still warm.

4   Just before it begins to freeze, after about 20 minutes, remove from the freezer and place in the refrigerator.

5   To serve, unwrap the octopus roll and slice across into rounds 3–5mm thick. Allowing 2–3 slices per person, arrange on serving plates and dress with the lemon juice and olive oil, then scatter with the chopped chives and dried miso.

note   An average whole octopus, as here, will produce 4 portions, and you can chop the head into bite-sized pieces and serve with the Ceviche Sauce on page 247.
   Rolling the octopus while still hot will help the tentacles stick together because of their gelatine content. The more the tentacles are pounded at the beginning, the more tender the finished result will be. Octopus usually requires salt, but here the dried miso takes its place.

Dublin Bay prawn sashimi

Dublin Bay prawns, also known as langoustines, scampi or Norwegian lobsters, have a wonderful sweet shellfish taste. Here we prepare them very simply in order to retain as much of the natural flavours as possible. Only live langoustines should be used for this dish in order to ensure the utmost freshness.

serves 1

2 live Dublin Bay prawns
1/2 lemon
2 tablespoons olive oil
sea salt and freshly ground black pepper
chive stalks, for garnish

1   Put the Dublin Bay prawns in the freezer for about 15 minutes, so they go into a deep sleep and won't be aware of the next stage.

2   Blanch the prawns for 10 seconds in boiling salted water and then plunge them into iced water to cool them down and stop the cooking process. Drain well.

3   With a large knife, cut right through the head and body, then cut through the tail, leaving the underside of the tail shell intact so the prawn opens in half like a book and the soft underside of tail shell is still joined together in the middle.

4   Lay the opened-out prawns on a serving dish and squeeze the lemon juice over the tail meat, followed by the olive oil. Season with salt and freshly ground black pepper, and garnish with chive stalks.

Fresh octopus sashimi with bottarga

In this dish, the texture and flavour of raw octopus are enhanced by the saltiness of the bottarga (see the note opposite) and the citrus juices. For a more detailed description of how to prepare octopus, see page 68.

Here, the suckers removed from the octopus's tentacles are used as an unusual and eye-catching garnish. You do need to clean these very carefully too, as described and shown opposite, as they can be very sandy.

serves 4

1 large fresh octopus tentacle
a little sea salt
1 piece of mullet bottarga
4 asparagus spears, peeled and blanched
1/2 teaspoon salt-packed baby capers, rinsed
1/4 teaspoon crushed black peppercorns
1 teaspoon yuzu juice (see page 253)
1 teaspoon lemon juice
1 teaspoon freshly milled black pepper

1 Remove the suckers from the octopus tentacle by cutting from the thickest end just below the skin. As you work the knife sideways, gradually remove the skin underneath the suckers along the length of the tentacle, then repeat the process for the remaining skin left all around the tentacle.

2 Place the skin with the suckers attached into a mortar and knead with a little salt to remove the slime and sand from inside the suckers.

3 Bring a pan of water with a pinch of salt to the boil and place the suckers in it. Boil for 5 minutes, remove and drain. Cut the suckers out of the skin and reserve.

4 Using a clean kitchen cloth, gently rub off the membrane of the skinned tentacle, then rinse it quickly in cold salted water and pat dry.

5 Slice the tentacle as thinly as possible, about 2–4mm thick, then slice the bottarga even more thinly (the bottarga is easier to slice).

6 Cut the asparagus spears to the same length as the octopus slices and, if they are more than 5mm thick, cut each in half lengthways.

7 Arrange 'sandwiches' consisting of a slice of asparagus followed by a slice of octopus, then a slice of bottarga, making sure they overlap one another, and repeat this process to make 8 'sandwiches' in total.

8 Place a reserved sucker on each slice of octopus, then sprinkle the capers, cracked black pepper and sea salt over the top. Mix the yuzu juice and lemon juice together, and drizzle this over the top.

note Bottarga (sometimes called the poor man's caviar) is the roe of the grey mullet (or tuna) which has been pressed and cured in sea salt for a few weeks. It is very popular in the Mediterranean as well as in Japan, and you may find it in Italian delis as well as Japanese stores.

Turbot sashimi with fried garlic, onion, jalapeño and matsuhisa dressing

The turbot sashimi is dressed with an interesting range of onion textures, from the soft sweet onions in the Matsuhisa Dressing to the chopped red onion and crispy garlic chips on the top.

serves 4

vegetable oil for frying
2–3 garlic cloves, thinly sliced
150g boneless skinless fresh turbot fillet
1 tablespoon finely chopped red onion
1 teaspoon finely chopped deseeded jalapeño pepper
Matsuhisa dressing (see page 242)

1   Bring about 2cm of oil in a saucepan to 150°C and slowly deep-fry the garlic slices until they turn a light golden brown. Remove immediately and drain on kitchen paper.

2   On a chopping board, place the turbot fillet with the skinned side up and the tail on the knife-hand side. Steadying the tail end with the fingers of the other hand, hold the knife so that the top is inclined sharply to the side away from the fish. Then, from the tail end, start cutting thin slices (2–3mm thick), keeping the blade at an acute angle to achieve a clean cut across the grain. Try to cut each slice of fish in one drawing stroke, letting the weight of the knife do the work as you pull back the blade.

3   Arrange the slices on a serving dish (you will need about 16 slices for 4 people) and spread the garlic chips across the top, followed by the red onion and the Jalapeño. Pour a little of the Matsuhisa dressing around the edges of the fish to finish.

note   This method of cutting the fish is called the *Usu Zukuri* technique in Japan, and can be used for any firm white fish such as snapper, sea bass and flounder. Obviously, be sure to have a really sharp knife for this and be careful with it when cutting the fish.

Umamijime tiradito

Here turbot has been marinated with both bonito and konbu to add lots more umami flavour to the raw fish. Lemon and yuzu juices then impart a wonderful citrus tang, and the chilli gives it bite.

serves 4

1 sheet of konbu (see page 251)
handful of bonito flakes (see page 250)
2 teaspoons sea salt
1 jalapeño pepper, deseeded and finely chopped
150g boneless skinless fresh turbot fillet
handful of coriander, stems removed
Rocoto chile paste (see page 252) or red chilli purée
2 tablespoons lemon juice
1 tablespoon yuzu juice (see page 253)

1   The day before, soak the konbu in cold water for 2 hours. Drain the soaked konbu and wipe it dry with a clean cloth, then cut it in half.

2   Mix the bonito flakes, salt and chopped jalapeño together and spread over both sides of the turbot fillet. Place the fillet on top of one of the pieces of konbu, then put the other half sheet over the top to make a sandwich with the turbot in the middle. Wrap in clingfilm and refrigerate overnight.

3   Next day, unwrap the turbot 'sandwich', remove the konbu and reserve. On a chopping board, place the turbot fillet with the skinned side up and the tail on the knife-hand side. Steadying the tail end with the fingers of the other hand, hold the knife so that the top is inclined sharply to the side away from the fish. Then, from the tail end, start cutting thin slices (2–3mm thick), keeping the blade at an acute angle to achieve a clean cut across the grain. Try to cut each slice the fish in one drawing stroke, letting the weight of the knife do the work as you pull back the blade.

4   Arrange the slices on a serving dish (you will need about 16 slices for 4 people) in a fan shape.

5   Roll the reserved konbu up into a cylinder and cut this across into strips as thinly as possible. Place these neatly at the base of the fanned turbot, then arrange the coriander leaves in between the konbu and the turbot. Put the tiniest dot of chile paste in the centre of each turbot slice. Mix the lemon and yuzu juices and pour this around the dish to finish.

notes   When eating this dish, take a leaf of coriander and a little konbu and eat with a slice of turbot.
   After the lemon and yuzu juices have been added, the dish must be eaten quickly as this fish will start to 'cook' if left for too long. If you can't find yuzu, use limes.

Toro miso with jalapeño salsa

Here the texture and flavour of the tuna belly are heightened by quickly searing the outside surfaces. The slices are then paired with the sweetness and acidity of a Yuzu miso dressing and the kick of Jalapeño salsa.

80g boneless skinless toro (tuna belly) in a block
freshly ground black pepper
2 tablespoons Jalapeño salsa (see page 243)
a few blanched skinned broad beans, for garnish

for the Yuzu miso sauce
15g yuzu rind (see page 253)
150ml Den miso (see page 244)
about 2 tablespoons rice vinegar

1   Make the Yuzu miso sauce: blend the yuzu rind to a pulp in a food processor and strain off the juice, pressing it to get as much out as you can. Mix this into the Den miso and then add just enough of the vinegar to get a consistency that will coat the back of a spoon.

2   Season the tuna with black pepper. Heat a non-stick frying pan until very hot and quickly sear each side of the tuna, making sure that all the outside has been completely seared and no red meat is visible. Plunge it immediately into iced water to stop the cooking process, then drain and pat dry with kitchen paper.

3   Flood the base of a serving dish with the Yuzu miso sauce. Slice the tuna across into slices about 3–5mm thick and arrange them overlapping in the centre of the plate. Spoon a little of the Jalapeño salsa over the top and garnish with the blanched skinned broad beans.

notes   Be sure to plunge the toro immediately into iced water after searing to prevent it overcooking.

To spread a sauce evenly around the base of a plate, put the sauce in the centre and carefully tilt the plate so it runs to the edges.

Toro hagashi

The beauty of this dish is the melt-in-the-mouth toro hagashi, which is essentially the flesh that is found in between the sinews of the tuna meat. This is quickly seared on one side and served with a medley of mushrooms, olives and capers.

serves 2

100g fresh toro (tuna belly)
sea salt and freshly ground black pepper
1 teaspoon garlic purée
2 fresh cep (porcini) mushrooms, sliced
4 morels, halved
olive oil for cooking
4 caper berries
2 stoned green olives, sliced
1 tablespoon fresh green peas, blanched
a little Yuzu dressing (see page 63)

1 From a piece of toro (tuna belly) remove the outer sinew on both sides as illustrated below. Season the tuna with sea salt and black pepper and rub one side with a little garlic purée.

2 Heat a non-stick frying pan until medium hot and quickly sear the garlic-rubbed side of the tuna. Remove from the pan and keep to one side.

3 In the same frying pan over a medium heat, sauté the cep and morel mushrooms in a little olive oil in until just cooked and softened.

4 Add the caper berries, sliced olives and peas, and toss for 30 seconds. Season with salt and pepper.

5 Place the tuna in the centre of a serving dish and neatly spoon the mushroom mixture over the top. Dress with a little Yuzu dressing to finish. This dish is best served slightly warm.

note As the toro hagashi meat is quite thin, make sure that it is quickly seared and removed from the heat, so as to retain the raw top side.

Duck tataki with wasabi salsa

Most people in the West associate sashimi with raw fish and seafood. In this dish, however, duck breast is seared to make the skin crispy and then given a fiery lift with a wasabi salsa and finished with vinegary ponzu. When choosing duck for this dish, do not use wild or well-hung birds – the meat should be very red and fresh.

serves 4

1 leek, trimmed and well rinsed
sea salt and freshly ground black pepper
1 fresh duck breast
1 teaspoon capers
1/3 recipe quantity Ponzu (see page 248)
1/2 sharon fruit, thinly sliced

for the salsa
2 teaspoons wasabi pickle (wasabi zuke, see page 253)
1 tablespoon finely chopped onion
1/2 teaspoon grated garlic
1 tablespoon grapeseed oil

1   Preheat the oven to 180°C/gas 4. Place the leek on a baking sheet and season with a little salt and pepper, then bake for 10–12 minutes, until slightly browned on the outside.

2   Trim any excess fat from the duck breast, leaving a thickness of only about 2–3mm. Gently score the remaining fat with a knife horizontally and vertically 5mm apart to produce a cross-hatch pattern on the fat, but do not cut through the fat into the meat.

3   Place a non-stick saucepan over a medium heat. Season the duck breast with salt and pepper and place it in the pan, skin side down. Cook for 1 minute, using a spatula to press the duck down so that all the fat comes in contact with pan, so that it will start to render and become crisp. Check after 1 minute to see if it is crisp; if not, cook for another 30 seconds. When crisp, quickly turn the breast over and sear all the remaining surfaces for a few seconds only, then remove the duck from the pan an leave to cool.

4   To make the salsa: in a small non-reactive bowl, mix together all the ingredients, then season with salt and pepper to taste.

5   Cut the cooled duck breast across into slices about 3mm thick and arrange them, overlapping one another, on a serving dish. Place a little of the wasabi salsa on each slice of duck breast.

6   Cut the leek into 5mm roundels and place one on the top of each slice of duck breast with a caper. Pour a little of the Ponzu around the slices of duck and garnish with a few slices of sharon fruit.

soup

Watercress and soya milk soup

This is a creamy watercress soup that uses soya milk instead of cream. It is therefore very light and healthy, as well as being quick to make, and in summer it is also good served cold.

serves 4

3 bunches of watercress
600ml Dashi (see page 250)
200ml unsweetened soya milk
4 tablespoons light soy sauce
salt and freshly ground black pepper

1 Pick the watercress from the stems and keep them separate, then roughly chop the stems.

2 In a large saucepan, bring the Dashi just to the boil, add the watercress stems and simmer for 5 minutes.

3 Pour the mixture into a blender and blend until smooth.

4 Strain the mixture back into the saucepan and add the soya milk. Bring the soup back to a gentle simmer and add the watercress leaves, reserving a few for garnish. Simmer for 3 minutes.

5 Blend again until smooth and strain into a clean saucepan. Bring back to the heat and add the soy sauce, then season to taste with salt and pepper.

6 Ladle into bowls and garnish with a few shredded watercress leaves.

note This treatment works equally well with other strong-tasting greens, such as spinach and sorrel.

Mushroom soup with truffle and jabugo

This delicate clear soup, scented with white truffles and Iberian ham, is first drunk out of small cups. The remaining solid contents are then eaten at the end, with chopsticks.

serves 4

50g shiitake mushrooms
50g oyster mushrooms
50g ceps
20g Jabugo or other Iberian ham, cut into fine strips
2–3g white truffle slices

for the stock
800ml Dashi (see page 17)
4 tablespoons sake
4 tablespoons light soy sauce
sea salt

1   Make the stock by mixing together the Dashi, sake and soy sauce with sea salt to taste, and warm slightly in a saucepan to dissolve the salt.

2   Divide each of the mushroom types evenly between 4 soup kettles and fill them with the stock mixture.

3   Put the kettles in a large steamer and steam for 12 minutes. This will allow the mushroom flavours to infuse slowly into the soup.

4   Add the ham and truffle slices to the soup and serve.

note   If you don't have soup kettles, you can just make the soup in a saucepan, but the heat must be kept very gentle and the soup should not boil.

Baked king crab soup

King crab is gently cooked in stock, accented by chilli garlic sauce and an assortment of mushrooms, then baked in the oven under a pastry topping. All the wonderful aromas of this soup are released when the pastry top is removed at the table. You'll need 4 suitably sized ovenproof bowls for this.

serves 4

400g puff pastry
flour for dusting
50g girolle mushrooms
50g shiitake mushrooms
50g oyster mushrooms
4 large king crab claws, shelled
1 egg, beaten

for the stock
800ml Dashi (see page 17)
4 tablespoons sake
4 tablespoons light soy sauce
2 teaspoons chilli garlic sauce (see page 250)
1/2 teaspoon sea salt

1 Preheat the oven to 180°C/gas 4.

2 Make the stock by mixing all the ingredients together in a saucepan and warm gently to dissolve the salt.

3 Roll the pastry out to a thickness of about 3mm and, using one of the ovenproof bowls as a guide, cut out 4 pastry circles to make 'lids' for the bowls. These should be large enough to provide a good overhang when in place.

4 Divide the mushrooms evenly between the 4 bowls, place the crab claws on top of the mushrooms and cover with the stock, leaving a 1–2cm gap from the top of the bowl.

5 Brush the rims of the bowls with the egg wash and, making sure that they overlap the rim sufficiently, place the pastry circles over the bowls and seal at the edges by pressing lightly. There is no need to trim too much from the sides as this will help keep the pastry circles tight on the top, so they don't sag into the soup. Brush the pastry tops lightly with the egg wash and make a tiny hole in the centre of each to allow steam to escape. Bake in the oven for 15–20 minutes, until the pastry has cooked and is risen and golden.

6 Serve just as it is, straight from the oven.

note Any assortment of mushrooms can be used, just pick your favourites.

Foie gras miso soup

Here miso soup is enriched with fresh foie gras and black truffles to produce a dish that is hearty and rich, but with a wonderful silky finish.

serves 4

60g fresh raw foie gras
400ml Dashi (see page 17)
50g white miso (see page 253)
1/2 teaspoon black truffle oil
4 slices of black truffle

1   Place the foie gras in the freezer for 20 minutes to get it nice and firm.

2   In a non-reactive saucepan, bring the Dashi to just below boiling point and whisk in the miso a little at a time, until completely dissolved.

3   Preferably using a mandolin, shave the chilled foie gras into the thinnest possible slices, so that they will liquefy in the soup.

4   Add the foie gras to the soup over the heat and whisk it in.

5   Add the truffle oil and blend the soup in a blender until smooth.

6   Pour into small soup cups and place a slice of truffle on the top of each one.

note   Once the foie gras has been added to the soup, it should not be kept hot for too long or it will eventually begin to separate.

Iberian pork cheek miso soup

Pork cheeks are a much favoured delicacy in Spain and those from the Iberian black pigs in Jabugo are particularly celebrated, almost as much as their world-renowned hams. As the muscles in the cheeks are well used, the delicious meat does tend to be very tough, so it needs long slow cooking.

serves 4

for the braised pork cheeks

4 Iberian pork cheeks as above
2 garlic cloves, peeled
1/2 teaspoon black peppercorns
2cm piece of ginger, peeled
1 bird's-eye chilli
2 tablespoons light soy sauce

for the soup

400ml Dashi (see page 17)
80g white miso paste (see page 253)
2 tablespoons sake
8 cooked baby carrots
8 cooked baby turnips
1/4 red chilli, thinly sliced
1/4 green chilli, thinly sliced
shredded daikon

1   Preheat the oven to 150°C/gas 2. Place the pork cheeks in a casserole dish, add the garlic, pepper, ginger, chilli and soy sauce, then cover with cold water. Cover the casserole with a lid or foil and braise in the oven for 1¹/₂–2 hours, until tender. Allow the cheeks to cool in the liquor, then remove the cheeks and strain the cooking liquor, reserving both.

2   Make the soup by bringing the Dashi and 400ml of the reserved cooking liquor to just below the boil and gently whisk in the white miso paste until dissolved. Stir in the sake and strain.

3   To serve: cut the cheeks into bite-sized pieces and reheat in some of the remaining cooking liquor. Heat the carrots and turnips quickly in boiling water. Divide the pieces of cheek and the vegetables evenly between 4 deep soup bowls and pour over the hot miso soup. Garnish with the sliced red and green chillies and shredded daikon.

note   There are many varieties of miso paste and they all have different levels of saltiness, so add to the soup in small amounts, tasting as you go.

fry

Mediterranean prawn tempura with jalapeño ponzu

One of the most popular dishes at all our restaurants is the Rock Shrimp Tempura. Here, we have used the same technique with Mediterranean red prawns, (*crevettes rouges, gamberi rossi*), which are large and wonderfully flavoured, almost like lobster. They are enlivened by a spicy Jalapeño ponzu.

serves 2

12 fresh Mediterranean red prawns
vegetable oil for deep-frying
handful of assorted salad leaves
small quantity of Yuzu dressing (see page 63)
4 tablespoons Jalapeño ponzu (see page 245)
chopped chives, to garnish

for the Tempura batter
200ml ice-cold water
1 egg yolk
100g plain flour

1   Prepare the prawns by removing the heads from the body and peeling the shell from the tail. Cut a small incision along the back and remove the dark vein or intestinal tract. Rinse under cold running water and drain.

2   Heat a medium-to-large pan of oil (8–10cm deep) to a temperature of 180°C.

3   Make the tempura batter: in a mixing bowl, mix the ice-cold water and the egg yolk, using a pair of chopsticks. Then add the flour, a little at a time, mixing it in with the chopsticks until it is all incorporated. Don't overwork it, or the batter will be heavy – aim for a loose batter that still has a few little lumps of unmixed flour.

4   In a serving bowl, dress the salad leaves with a little of the Yuzu dressing, then place in a large serving dish. Put the Jalapeño ponzu in a small dipping cup.

5   One at a time, dip the prawns into the cold tempura batter, allow any excess batter to run off and gently place into the hot oil. Cook for 1–2 minutes until lightly coloured and crisp, then remove with a draining spoon and drain on kitchen paper.

6   Once they are all cooked, place the prawns on the salad leaves and sprinkle with chopped chives. Serve with the dipping cup of Jalapeño ponzu.

notes   Using chopsticks will prevent the batter becoming overworked; a loose batter that still has lumps of unmixed flour will help to make a lighter crisper batter. Ensure that the water is very cold and that you prepare the batter just before cooking, as this will also help to make the finished results crisp.
   If you can't find Mediterranean red prawns, you could use tiger or Dublin Bay prawns. For the salad you can use any mixture of greens as you prefer, but be sure you dress the salad only just before you cook the prawns.

Rock shrimp kakiage with Parmesan

Parmesan cheese adds another dimension of flavour to this wonderfully crisp *kakiage* – the Japanese term for a mixed tempura. Using a spatula or fish slice helps stop the *kakiage* breaking into pieces when it is first placed in the hot oil. When it has set as one piece, it can be gently removed from the spatula to continue cooking.

serves 2

vegetable oil for deep-frying
1 spring onion
120g rock shrimp or chopped tiger prawns
25g sliced white onion
50g freshly grated Parmesan cheese
Tempura batter (see page 99)
chopped parsley, for garnish
sea salt and freshly ground black pepper
1/2 lemon

1   Heat a medium-to-large pan of oil (8–10cm deep) to a temperature of 180°C.

2   Chop the spring onion into 5mm lengths and place in a mixing bowl with the shrimp or prawns, onion and 40g of the grated Parmesan. Pour the tempura batter a little at a time into the mixing bowl so that the contents are bound with the batter but are slightly loose in the mixture, then divide the mixture between 2 small cups or bowls.

3   Immerse a perfectly dry metal spatula or fish slice horizontally into the hot oil so that it is about 2cm just below the surface. Pour the contents from the first bowl carefully on to the spatula. As it begins to cook, slowly immerse it into the oil, so that it stays in one piece. After about 20–30 seconds, slide it off the spatula with a palette knife or something similar and cook for 3–4 minutes, turning it regularly until crisp and cooked completely through. Remove from the oil and drain on kitchen paper. Repeat the whole process with the contents of the second bowl.

4   Place the cooked *kakiage* on a serving dish and sprinkle with the remaining Parmesan and the chopped parsley. Serve with the sea salt, black pepper and a lemon quarter on the side. Eat while still hot and crisp.

Turbot tempura

Slices of turbot are quickly fried in tempura batter to give a crisp texture on the outside while remaining deliciously soft on the inside, doing superb justice to the wonderfully flavoured lean firm flesh of the fish.

serves 4

120g skinless boneless fresh turbot fillet
vegetable oil for deep-frying
tempura flour for dusting
Tempura batter (see page 99)
1/2 red onion, thinly sliced
picked coriander leaves
a small quantity of Ama zu ponzu (see page 249)

1   Place the turbot fillet on a chopping board with the skinned side up and the tail on the side of your preferred hand. Steadying the other end of the turbot with the fingers of your other hand, hold the knife in your preferred hand, so that the top is inclined sharply away from the fish. From the tail end of the fillet, start cutting fairly thick slices (5mm), keeping the blade at that acute angle to achieve a clean cut across the grain.

2   Heat a medium-to-large pan of oil (8–10cm deep) to a temperature of 180°C. Dust the slices of turbot in a little tempura flour and shake off any excess. Then dip them into the cold tempura batter, allowing any excess batter to run off, and gently place in the hot oil, one at a time. Cook in 2 or 3 batches for 1–2 minutes each, until light and crisp. Remove with a draining spoon and drain on kitchen paper.

3   Transfer the tempura fish to a serving dish, piling the pieces on top of one another and scatter over the sliced onion and a few coriander leaves. Pour the Ama zu ponzu into the bottom of the plate and consume while still hot and crisp.

notes   This recipe is good for all firm white fish, such as sea bass, brill, sole, plaice and lemon sole.
    The cooked tempura should be eaten fairly quickly after cooking, as the batter will soften due to the hot steam coming from the cooked fish flesh inside.

Caviar tempura

This contrast of the crisp texture of the batter and the delicious saltiness of the caviar, finished with a squeeze of lemon juice, makes a truly mouth-watering morsel. The first time you try this, it may be easier to use monkfish, as it has a much firmer flesh and will be more forgiving.

serves 4

150g skinless boneless sea bass fillet
4 teaspoons Oscietra caviar
vegetable oil for deep-frying
tempura flour for dusting
Tempura batter (see page 99)
1 lemon, halved and thickly sliced

1   Place the sea bass fillet on a chopping board with the skinned side up and the tail on the side of your preferred hand. Steadying the other end of the sea bass with the fingers of the other hand, hold the knife in your preferred hand so that the top is inclined sharply away from the fish. From the opposite end of the fillet, start cutting slices about 8mm thick, keeping the blade at that acute angle, so as to achieve slices with a width of about 2.5cm (you will need 8 good slices).

2   With the tip of a small sharp knife, carefully cut a slit in one end of each slice of sea bass so that it forms a pocket inside the slice; slowly work the knife tip in, to make the pocket as large as possible without creating any holes. Fill each pocket with about $1/2$ teaspoon of caviar per slice, making sure that the caviar is pushed well inside (the handle of a teaspoon is good for this). Secure the slit end of the slice with a cocktail stick, pushing it through and then back again so that the caviar is sealed inside.

3   Heat a medium-to-large pan of oil (8–10cm deep) to a temperature of 180°C. Carefully dust the stuffed sea bass slices in a little tempura flour and shake off any excess. Then, one at a time, dip them into the cold tempura batter, allow any excess batter to run off and gently place them in the hot oil. Cook for 1–2 minutes, until the batter is light and crisp. Lift out with a draining spoon and drain on kitchen paper.

4   To serve, place each slice on a serving spoon and serve with the lemon slices to squeeze over the top.

Whole spiny lobster three ways

Here spiny lobster is prepared in three different ways, as ceviche, sashimi and tempura. A suitably grand way to serve a whole spiny lobster, it is well worth the end result. You can also make this dish with an ordinary lobster, using the blanched claws for the tempura part of the dish.

serves 4–6

1 whole live spiny lobster
salt
iced water
1 lime

for the New-style spiny lobster ceviche
1/2 garlic clove, puréed
1 tablespoon finely shredded ginger
handful of chive stalks
a little fresh aloe vera, thinly sliced
2 tablespoons Yuzu soy (see page 248)
2 tablespoons New-style oil (see page 245)
pinch of white sesame seeds

for the Spiny lobster with Sansho pepper salsa
1 teaspoon green Sansho peppercorns (see page 252)
1 teaspoon deseeded and finely chopped red chilli
50g white onion, finely chopped
1 tablespoon olive oil
2 tablespoons lemon juice
1/3 teaspoon salt

for the Spiny lobster tempura with creamy spicy sauce
vegetable oil for deep-frying
Tempura batter (see page 99)
small quantity of Creamy spicy sauce (see page 246)
1 tablespoon chopped chives

1   Put the lobster in the freezer for 20 minutes, so it goes into a deep sleep and won't be aware of the next stage.

2   Bring to the boil a saucepan of salted water large enough to cover the lobster. Plunge the lobster head first into the water for 1 minute. Remove the lobster and plunge it into a bowl of iced water to cool. This will enable the meat to be more easily removed from the shell.

3   Remove the tail from the body and carefully cut open the tail shell with a pair of scissors, then gently remove the tail meat. Starting at the thinner end, cut two-thirds of the tail meat into slices 2mm thick, and then cut the remaining piece into 5mm dice. If you like, you can reserve the lobster feelers and some shell for garnish.

4   To make the New-style Spiny Lobster Ceviche, lay one-third of the lobster slices flat on a suitable serving dish. Dab the slices with a little garlic purée and sprinkle the ginger and chives evenly on top. Then add a few slices of aloe vera before spooning the Yuzu soy over the top.

5   Heat a small pan with the New-style Oil until it just begins to smoke and then pour over the lobster slices to sear the top. Finish by sprinkling with the sesame seeds.

6   To make the Spiny Lobster with Sansho Pepper Salsa, put the remaining tail meat slices in a suitable dish, mix all the other ingredients together and spoon this Sansho Pepper salsa over the top.

7   To make the Spiny Lobster Tempura, heat a medium-to-large pan of oil (8–10cm deep) to a temperature of 180°C. Dip the diced lobster into the cold tempura batter, allowing any excess batter to run off, and then gently place into the hot oil. Cook for 1–2 minutes, until light and crisp, then remove and drain on kitchen paper. Place in a bowl and quickly mix with the Creamy spicy sauce while still hot. Serve sprinkled with chopped chives.

8   Arrange the three separate dishes on a large serving platter and garnish with a lime cut in half, together with the lobster feelers and some shell, if you like.

Sea urchin tempura London-style

These delicate little parcels of sea urchin are actually wrapped in puff pastry and then quickly fried to encapsulate the full flavour of the sea.

serves 2

about 150g puff pastry
2 shiso leaves (see page 253)
1 teaspoon wasabi paste (see page 253)
100g sea urchin
vegetable oil for deep-frying

for the garnish
sea salt
shichimi togarashi (see page 252)
¹/₂ lime

1   Roll out the puff pastry thinly (to a thickness of 1–2mm) and, using a round 5cm pastry cutter, cut out 4 circles.

2   Place half a shiso leaf on each puff pastry circle and spread a little of the wasabi in the centre of each one. Divide the sea urchin evenly between them and close the puff pastry up around it, sealing at the top to form a small purse shape.

3   Heat a medium-to-large pan of oil (8–10cm deep) to a temperature of 180°C and fry the purses for 1–2 minutes until puffed and crispy on the outside.

4   Line a suitable dish with paper and place the well-drained purses on to it. Serve with sea salt, shichimi togarashi and the half lime on the side.

note   Care must be taken when sealing the purses to make sure that there are no gaps where oil might get inside during cooking.

Sea bass and truffle rolls

Here crisp spring rolls are filled with sea bass infused with the scented aroma of fresh white truffle.

serves 4

160g boneless sea bass fillet
2 large spring roll wrappers
1 egg, beaten
3g white truffle, thinly sliced
sea salt and freshly ground black pepper
vegetable oil for deep-frying
shichimi togarashi (see page 252)
a little karashi su miso (see page 251)

1   Skin the sea bass fillet, reserving the skin for later. Cut the sea bass evenly into 4 pieces.

2   Working with 1 spring roll wrapper at a time, cut the sheet diagonally in half and place one piece on a flat surface with the point of the triangle away from you. Egg wash all the edges. Place a piece of sea bass and a few slices of the truffle in the middle of the edge nearest to you and season with salt and pepper. Fold first the left and then the right side of each wrapper into the centre over the sea bass, then roll the whole thing away from you, making sure the edges are completely sealed. Repeat the process to make 3 more rolls. Care should be taken that the rolls are completely sealed at the edges, otherwise the oil will get inside the roll during cooking.

3   Place a non-stick frying pan over a medium heat. Pressing it down with a metal spatula or fish slice, cook the reserved sea bass skin in the dry pan, turning it occasionally until it becomes crisp.

4   Heat a medium-to-large pan of oil (8–10cm deep) to a temperature of 180°C and fry the rolls in two batches in the hot oil for 3–4 minutes each batch, until golden brown. Lift them out with a draining spoon and drain on kitchen paper.

5   Serve on a suitable dish, sprinkled with the remaining truffle slices. Place the crispy sea bass skin on top and serve more salt and black pepper, shichimi togarashi and karashi su miso separately.

Spanish mackerel nanban-zuke

Here mackerel fillets are fried whole twice to get a really crisp exterior, then served with a sauce made from cider vinegar, soy sauce and mirin to cut through the oiliness of the fish.

serves 2

vegetable oil, for deep-frying

2 boneless mackerel fillets, each about 100g

salt

arrowroot for dusting

4 whole spring onions, trimmed

4 fresh coriander leaves on the stem

4 fresh flat parsley leaves on the stem

Ito-Togarashi (see page 251), for garnish

for the sauce

pinch of shichimi togarashi (see page 252)

1 teaspoon sea salt

5 tablespoons cider vinegar

3 tablespoons mirin (see page 252)

3 tablespoons light soy sauce

200ml Dashi (see page 17)

50g fresh root ginger, roughly chopped

1   First make the sauce: put all the ingredients together in a non-reactive saucepan and place over a low heat. Bring to just below boiling point, strain and keep warm.

2   Heat a medium-to-large pan of oil (8–10cm deep) to a temperature of 180°C. Season the mackerel fillets with salt and dust in the arrowroot, then fry in the hot oil for 2–3 minutes. Remove and allow to drain on kitchen paper. Then repeat the process again, frying them for another 2–3 minutes, and drain.

3   Next, fry the whole spring onions for 30 seconds (make sure that they are completely dry before placing them in the hot oil). Remove and allow to drain.

4   Add the coriander and parsley stems to the hot sauce for a few seconds to let them soften.

5   Place the mackerel fillets in a shallow bowl and pour a little of the sauce around them. Arrange the coriander and parsley, and the fried spring onion on the top of the fish. Garnish with the Ito-Togarashi and serve hot.

note   It is important that the sauce should not boil, otherwise it will become too intense in flavour.

Fish and chips Nobu-style

Perfect party food – fish and chips all in one piece!

serves 6–8

1kg unpeeled Spunta or other good frying potatoes
1kg cod, filleted and skinned
sea salt and freshly ground black pepper
50g butter, softened
katakuriko (see page 251), for dusting
olive oil for frying
malt vinegar to serve

1   Start preparing this the day before you want to serve
it. Steam the potatoes until half-cooked, about 10
minutes, and allow them to cool. When cool, peel them,
then carefully cut them into slices about 1.5cm thick.

2   Season the cod with a little salt and place in a
colander for about 15 minutes to allow some of the excess
water from the fish to drain away, then rinse under cold
running water and pat completely dry.

3   Preheat the oven to 170°C/gas 3¹/2. Brush the inside
of a 23cm terrine with the softened butter, then line it
with clingfilm, making sure that you have plenty of
clingfilm overhanging the edges to cover the top of the
filling.

4   Cut the potato slices to the same width as the terrine
and place them in the bottom, making sure that it is
completely covered. Season with salt and pepper. Trim
the cod fillet to the same shape as the terrine, making
sure that it is around 1.5cm thick (you will need 2 pieces
like this) and lay on top of the potato, repeat potato and
cod layers and finish with a third layer of potato. Wrap
the clingfilm over the top to seal everything, then put the
lid on the terrine.

5   Place the terrine in a deep roasting pan filled with
boiling water, then put that in the oven and cook for 30
minutes. Test to see if the terrine is cooked by placing a
metal skewer into the centre. If it is easily pierced and the
tip of the skewer is hot when withdrawn, it is ready.

6   Remove the lid and allow the terrine to cool for 20
minutes, then place some weights on the top to press the
terrine (cans of beans or tomatoes, etc. are good for this).
Place in the refrigerator for a minimum of 24 hours to
allow it to set completely.

7   Next day, dip the terrine briefly into warm water,
then carefully turn it out on a clean board and remove all
the cling film. With a sharp knife, carefully cut the terrine
into thick slices (about 2cm). Then cut these into fat 'chip'
shapes.

8   Dust the slices in katakuriko and fry in some olive oil
in a non-stick pan until crisp and brown. Remove and drain
on kitchen paper.

9   Serve these 'chips' on pieces of paper with sea salt
and malt vinegar on the side.

note   For the terrine to be firm enough to slice properly
it must be pressed well, so don't be frightened to put too
much weight on it. The heavier the weight, the better the
pressing.

Savoy cabbage steak salad

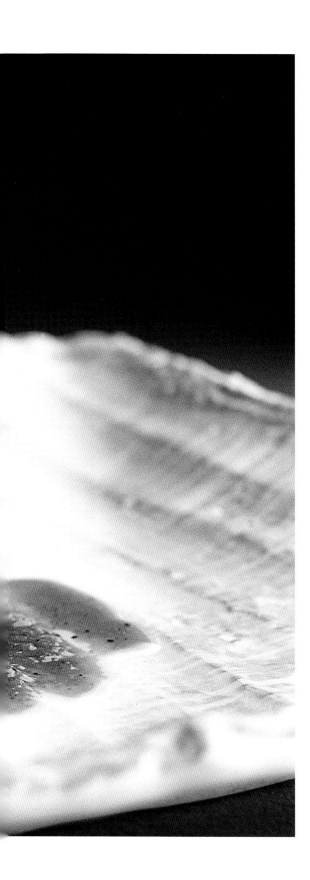

When cooking this dish, the sugars in the cabbage caramelize, giving it a wonderful flavour. It's even better when it's accompanied with the Matsuhisa Dressing.

serves 4

1 large head of savoy cabbage
sea salt and freshly ground black pepper
bowl of iced water
olive oil for cooking
1 garlic clove, thinly sliced
Matsuhisa dressing (see page 242)
25g shredded daikon (see page 250)

1   Cut off and discard the stalk end of the cabbage, then separate the leaves. Blanch these quickly in boiling salted water for 20 seconds. Refresh in iced water and drain well.

2   Spread out a sheet of foil about 45x20cm. Pile the cabbage leaves on the foil on top of one another, starting with the largest first and alternating the direction of the leaves so that they lie flat and maintain an even thickness. When assembled the leaves should look balanced. Roll them up in the foil, from the edge, firmly pressing down as you roll. The roll should form a cylinder about 10cm in diameter. Secure the foil around the rolled cabbage with string at intervals about 5cm apart. Cut the foil-wrapped roll in between the strings into cylinders about 5cm long.

3   Heat a frying pan with some olive oil in it and season the open ends of the cabbage with a generous amount of sea salt and fry them, one open end down, adding the sliced garlic to flavour the oil. Turn them over after 3–4 minutes and cook the other sides. The cabbage rolls are ready when both ends are lightly caramelized.

4   Cut the string and remove the foil. Pile the cylinders on a serving plate, cooked sides upwards, and dress with the Matsuhisa dressing and a little shredded daikon.

bake

Wood-roasted vegetables

Wood-roasted baby vegetables are combined with yuzu juice and miso to accentuate their smoky flavour. We have a new wood-fired oven in Nobu Berkeley Street and this is one of the dishes devised specially for it. If you don't have access to one, you can use a conventional oven or grill the vegetables on a charcoal barbecue first, before placing them in a conventional oven, to create the smoky effect.

serves 2

1 small bunch of yellow French beans, blanched
4 slices of sweet potato
4 broccoli florets
2 shiitake mushrooms
2 porcini mushrooms
1/2 bunch of enoki mushrooms
4 baby sweetcorn
2 baby courgettes
4 baby tomatoes
1/2 head of chicory, cut into quarters lengthways
2 slices of lotus root (see page 251)
1 garlic clove, thinly sliced
a little olive oil
sea salt and freshly ground black pepper
4 tablespoons Yuzu miso sauce (see page 78)

1 Preheat a wood-fired or pizza oven to 200°C/gas 6. Trim any vegetables that are large, so that everything is roughly the same size, and place in a bowl. Mix in the garlic slices. Lightly dress with a little olive oil and season with salt and pepper.

2 Arrange the coated vegetables neatly in a shallow ovenproof casserole or earthenware dish and bake in the oven for 10 minutes.

3 Drizzle the Yuzu miso sauce over the top and serve in the cooking dish.

note You may use any variety of vegetables or mushrooms for this dish as long as they have similar cooking times. If using any large root vegetables, they must first be blanched and cut into suitable sizes.

Baked aubergine with bonito and dashi ponzu

In this elegantly simple dish, the smoky flavours of roasted aubergine and the bonito flakes are enhanced with ginger soy sauce and rice vinegar.

serves 4

1 long aubergine
small handful of bonito flakes (see page 250)
5 tablespoons Dashi ponzu (see page 244)
1 tablespoon grated fresh root ginger

1   Preheat the oven to 230°C/gas 8. Cut the aubergine in half and then into quarters lengthways and place on a metal baking sheet or similar. Cook in the oven for 5 minutes until the skin is browned and the flesh is soft.

2   Place the baked aubergine on a chopping board and, while it is still hot, cut into bite-sized pieces. Transfer to a suitable serving dish, shaping it to look like the original aubergine again.

3   Sprinkle the bonito flakes over the top. Pour the Dashi ponzu into a dipping cup and place this on the dish, together with a small mound of grated ginger.

4   To eat, mix a little of the grated ginger into the Dashi Ponzu and then dip the pieces of aubergine into the sauce.

note   When the aubergine is hot and you sprinkle the bonito flakes on top, the rising heat from the aubergine will make the bonito flakes move and dance as if they were in the wind.

Baked mushrooms

This is a great way to enjoy all types of mushroom, baked and flavoured with sake, olive oil and yuzu juice. You can vary the types of mushroom that are used in this dish to suit your taste or availability.

serves 4

50g morels
50g button mushrooms
50g eringe mushrooms
50g ceps
2 tablespoons olive oil
2 garlic cloves, sliced
2 tablespoons sake
sea salt and freshly ground black pepper
1 tablespoon yuzu juice (see page 253) or lemon juice
1/2 red chilli, deseeded and thinly sliced

1   Preheat the oven to 230°C/gas 8. Wipe and clean the mushrooms (the morels may need to soaked to remove any sand or stiffly brushed, see note below). Cut any larger ones into evenly sized pieces, but try to keep the mushrooms whole if possible.

2   Place the mushrooms, olive oil, garlic and sake in an ovenproof earthenware pot or casserole dish with a tight-fitting lid. Season with sea salt and pepper and mix well to ensure all the mushrooms are coated. Cover tightly.

3   Bake in the oven for 12 minutes.

4   Remove the lid, add the yuzu juice and mix in. Sprinkle with the sliced chilli and serve.

note   Because of their pitted surface, a good way of cleaning morels without soaking them is to use a small stiff brush, like a nail brush.

Baked cabbage with white truffle

This dish is a new addition to the menu in one of our London restaurants and has been an instant success. The outer cabbage leaves become slightly sweet when they brown in the oven and the addition of truffles makes this a real earthy dish.

serves 4–6

1 head of pointed (summer) cabbage
4 tablespoons sake
4 tablespoons clarified butter (see note, right)
sea salt and freshly ground black pepper
shichimi togarashi (see page 252)
1 white truffle, sliced

1 Preheat the oven to 230°C/gas 8. Peel off the tough outer leaves from the cabbage and discard. Wash the remaining cabbage and drain. Cut the cabbage in half lengthways and then cut each half lengthways into 3 equal segments.

2 Place the cabbage wedges on a shallow baking dish or tray and pour over the sake and the clarified butter. Season with sea salt and black pepper, and cover the tray tightly with foil.

3 Bake in the oven for 8 minutes, then remove the tray, take off the foil and return the tray to the oven. Bake for a further 3–4 minutes, so the outside cabbage leaves begin to brown and caramelize.

4 Remove the cabbage wedges from the tray with a spatula or palette knife and place on a suitable serving dish. Spoon the juices from the tray over the cabbage, sprinkle a little shichimi togarashi on top and slice the white truffle over the top.

notes You can use dried red chilli instead of the shichimi and replace the white truffle with black truffle or even just a few drops of truffle oil – it even taste great just on its own. In the restaurant, we do this in a wood-fired oven, but a conventional oven or a salamander is perfectly adequate.

To clarify butter, heat it very gently in a small pan and skim off the foam that gathers on the top. After a minute or two, very gently pour off the clear liquid, leaving any milk solids behind. The butter can now be heated without burning so readily.

Salt-baked abalone

Baking them in a salt crust retains and enhances the full natural flavours of the sea in the abalone. The blanched cabbage leaves really just serve to hold the salt crust in place around the abalone.

serves 2

2 whole fresh abalone
200g fine salt
2 large cabbage leaves
white of 1 egg
small quantity of Yuzu miso sauce (see page 78)
1/2 lemon, halved and cut into thick slices

1   Preheat the oven to 200°C/gas 6. Extract the abalone from its shell and remove any dirt or debris. Cut away the hard projecting black sections around the edge and rinse under cold water. Scrub the abalone shells to remove any debris inside and out, then boil the shells in salted water for 10 minutes.

2   Blanch the cabbage leaves in another pan of salted boiling water for 30 seconds and drain.

3   Place the salt in a mixing bowl, then mix in just enough egg white to moisten it and create a fairly dry paste.

4   Cover each abalone completely with the salt mixture and wrap each one in a cabbage leaf to help hold the salt in place.

5   Bake in the oven for 30 minutes, then remove. Allow to cool for 5 minutes before taking off the cabbage leaves and the salt crust.

6   Cut each abalone into slices 5mm thick and dress back in their shells. Place on a dish, spoon a little Yuzu miso over each and serve with the lemon slices.

note   Use small-to-medium sized abalone for this dish.

Baby squid with ginger salsa

Here a quick blast in a very hot oven with baby vegetables and ginger gives a new dimension of flavour to baby squid. They require only the briefest of baking to be perfectly cooked.

serves 2

8 baby courgettes
olive oil for brushing
6 or 7 baby tomatoes
100g cleaned fresh baby squid
sea salt and freshly ground black pepper
4 tablespoons Ginger salsa (see page 243)

1   Preheat a hot grill or barbecue. Lightly brush the courgettes with olive oil and grill or barbecue for 2 minutes, turning them halfway, and allow to cool.

2   Preheat the oven to 230°C/gas 8. Place the tomatoes, squid and courgettes in a bowl and season with sea salt and pepper and a little olive oil. Put all the ingredients in an ovenproof ceramic dish or similar and spoon the Ginger salsa over the top.

3   Bake for 5 minutes and serve straight from the oven.

note   Try to pick evenly sized squid so that they will cook in the same time; if some are much larger than the rest, cut them into smaller pieces.

Razor clams cooked with celery, cucumber and olive oil

Here the clams are simply baked, shelled and tossed with a crunchy cucumber, olive and celery salad, lifted with an olive oil, sake and soy sauce dressing.

The dish is delightfully finished with the rich flavour and extra textural delight of a sprinkling of mouth-popping salmon eggs.

serves 2

6 live razor clams
2 tablespoons diced celery
2 tablespoons diced cucumber
1 tablespoons diced stoned green olives
2 tablespoons salmon eggs

for the dressing
3 tablespoons olive oil
$1/2$ teaspoon sea salt
2 tablespoons Sake soy (see page 248)
1 teaspoon freshly ground black pepper

1   Preheat the oven to 200°C/gas 6. Rinse the clams well under cold running water to remove any sand and place on a metal baking sheet.

2   Mix the diced celery, cucumber and olives together in a bowl.

3   In another bowl, combine the dressing ingredients.

4   Roast the clams in the oven for 5 minutes, then remove and leave to cool.

5   When they are cool enough to handle, remove the meat from the shells, discarding any clams that have not opened. On a chopping board, remove the tip of the siphon, the gills and digestive tract (the dark parts of the clam) with a knife and discard. Cut the flesh roughly into 3cm pieces and add to the bowl of diced celery, cucumber and olives. Toss together with the dressing.

6   Spoon on to a serving dish and sprinkle the salmon eggs on top to serve.

note   Make sure that the razor clams are live when they go into the oven and discard any that fail to open.

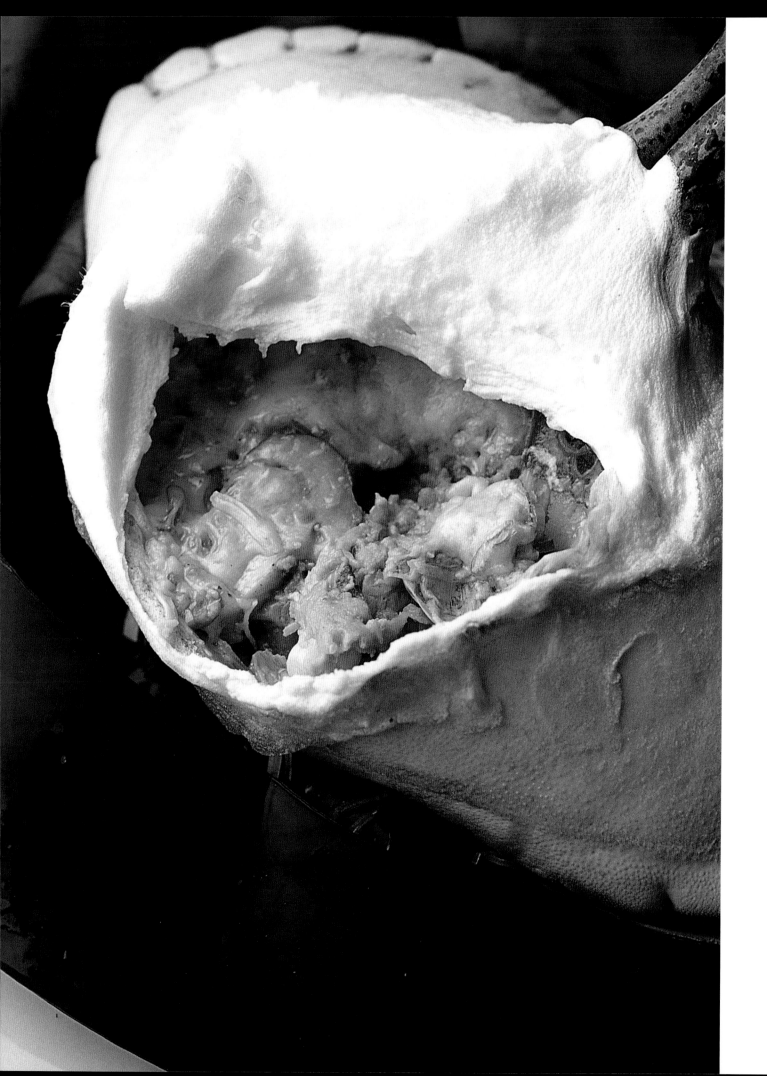

Frothing Cornish crab

Here steamed Cornish crab meat is returned to its shell and dressed with sea urchin and Parmesan cheese, then covered in egg white and fried. The egg white froths and resembles the bubbles that come from a live crab. This technique is called *koura-age* by the Japanese.

serves 2

1 large live (or freshly cooked) crab, preferably Cornish
2 tablespoons masago (smelt roe, see page 251)
sea salt and freshly ground black pepper
50g sea urchin, chopped
50g porcini mushrooms, sliced
2 tablespoons chopped spring onion
2 tablespoons grated Parmesan cheese
whites of 2 eggs
vegetable oil for deep-frying
seaweed for garnish

1   If the crab is live, steam or boil it for 20 minutes over high heat. Remove from the water or steamer and allow to drain and cool. When it is cool enough to handle, remove the legs and claws from the body, then crack the claws and the legs and remove all the white meat, putting it into a bowl. Be careful not to leave any small bits of shell in the meat.

2   Place the shell body on its back and remove the central body part (the piece where the legs were attached) from the shell. Using a chopstick, remove any white meat from the leg joints and add to the claw crab meat. With a spoon, scoop out the soft brown meat only and add to the bowl, then remove all remaining parts from inside the shell and discard. Rinse out the shell with water and drain.

3   Add the smelt roe to the crab meat and season with salt and pepper. Add a layer of the mixed crab meat to the shell, covering the whole cavity inside, and then put a layer of sea urchin on top. Cover the sea urchin with a layer of sliced mushrooms, then the chopped spring onion and finally the Parmesan cheese.

4   Beat the egg whites in a clean bowl until they form stiff peaks, then cover all the filling inside the crab shell with the beaten egg white and smooth over the top with a palette knife.

5   Bring about 4cm of oil in a shallow pan to 170°C. Slip the shell carefully into the oil, egged side up, and cook for 10 minutes, until the beaten egg white puffs up. Carefully remove and place on a suitable serving dish.

6   Dress with the seaweed and serve immediately.

notes   During cooking, make sure the height of the oil is no more than the height of the shell. The oil should not be so high that it gets inside the shell from the top.
    By the time the egg whites begin to froth and cook, the crab filling inside will be thoroughly heated through.

Roasted toro collar steak

Rich and juicy toro (tuna) collar is roasted quickly in the oven and then simply served with a spicy lemon, soy and vinegar sauce to cut through the oiliness of the tuna flesh.

serves 2

1 tablespoon grated daikon (see page 250)
1 teaspoon red chilli purée
2 tuna collar steaks, each about 150g
olive oil for brushing
sea salt and freshly ground black pepper
1 tablespoon shredded spring onion
1 tablespoon grated green mooli
Ponzu (see page 248)
2 pickled ginger stems (hajikami, see page 251)

1   Preheat the oven to 200°C/gas 6.

2   Mix together the grated daikon and the red chilli purée in a small bowl and set aside.

3   Brush the tuna steaks with olive oil, season with salt and pepper, and place on a flat metal roasting tray.

4   Cook in the oven for 8–10 minutes, depending on the thickness of the steaks.

5   Transfer to a serving dish and place the daikon and chilli mixture, the shredded spring onion and the grated green mooli in 3 neat little piles on the dish, along with the dipping bowl of Ponzu. Serve while still hot, garnished with the ginger stems.

notes   The tuna collar steaks are cut from the head and have a high fat content, rather like that of tuna belly, which is actually best suited to this dish.

When eating this, place a little of the grated daikon, chilli mix and spring onion into the dipping sauce with it.

Crispy-skin poussin

The baby chicken is cooked quickly in a hot oven to crisp up the skin nicely and it is then drenched in Spicy lemon dressing. It can be cooked without the cabbage stuffing, but it should then be cooked flat on a baking tray and the cooking time reduced by about 5 minutes.

serves 2

1 whole poussin (baby chicken)
sea salt and freshly ground black pepper
1/4 pointed (summer) cabbage, finely shredded
olive oil for brushing
1 whole head of chicory
3 cherry tomatoes
3 tablespoons Spicy lemon dressing (see page 242)
1/4 lemon

1   Preheat the oven to 200°C/gas 6.

2   Place the poussin, breast side down, on a chopping board and cut through the skin down to the bone in the middle of its back. Making small cuts, remove the meat away from the either side of the carcass. Cut the wing and leg joints at the knuckle and separate from the carcass, then remove the wishbone and continue cutting away the breasts from the breast bone to leave the carcass completely separate from the breasts and leg. Bone out the thigh bones from the legs, keeping the leg and breast meat still attached together in one whole piece.

3   Season the inside of the bird and the shredded cabbage with salt and pepper. Place the cabbage in the centre of the bird and wrap the sides of the bird around the cabbage so they overlap. Place on a baking tray, then brush lightly with olive oil and season.

4   Cut the chicory into quarters lengthways and brush them and the whole cherry tomatoes with olive oil. Season.

5   Place the poussin on a baking tray and cook in the oven for 15 minutes, then add the cherry tomatoes and chicory, and roast for a further 10 minutes.

6   Place the poussin on a suitable serving dish and garnish with the chicory and cherry tomatoes. Spoon over the Spicy lemon dressing and garnish with lemon wedges.

steam

Razor clams three ways

Here we cook razor clams in three different ways and serve them alongside one another. The contrasts of different textures and flavours this provides makes for a very exciting dish.

In case any clams turn out to be dead and so don't open when cooked, it may be good idea to buy one or two extra.

serves 2

6 live razor clams
salt

for the creamy spicy clams
2 teaspoons masago (smelt roe, see page 251)
2 teaspoons finely shredded spring onion
small quantity of Creamy spicy sauce (see page 245)

for the black bean sauce clams
1 tablespoon sake
2 teaspoons black bean sauce
1 tablespoon finely shredded ginger

for the new-style clams
1 tablespoon Sake soy (see page 248)
1 teaspoon garlic purée
1 tablespoon finely shredded root ginger
1 tablespoon chive batons
2 tablespoons New-style oil (see page 245)

1 Soak the clams overnight in plenty of cold water with a little salt; this will help to remove any sand from their digestive tracts.

2 Bring a pan of salted water to the boil and put in the clams for 30 seconds, then remove and refresh under cold running water. Discard any that have not opened.

3 Remove the clam meat from the shells and cut away the stomach (this is the dark part), then cut each one at an angle into 3–4 pieces. Arrange the pieces in the 6 best-looking half-shells and discard the rest.

4 For the creamy spicy clams, preheat a hot salamander or grill and grill 2 of the filled half-shells for 3 minutes until cooked. Spread with the masago and spring onion and cover with the creamy spicy sauce, then grill again until the sauce just begins to brown.

5 For the black bean clams, prepare a steamer or pan with a tight-fitting lid, a little water in the bottom and a plate to hold the clams out of the water. Take 2 more filled half-shells, pour the sake over them and spread a teaspoon of black bean sauce on each one, followed by a little shredded ginger, and steam them for 3 minutes.

6 For the new-style clams, take the remaining 2 filled half-shells, pour over the Sake soy and steam them for 3 minutes. When cooked, rub the clam meat with the garlic purée and place the ginger and chives on top. Heat the New-style oil in a small pan until it just begins to smoke, and immediately pour over the top of the clams.

7 To serve, arrange the three different types of clam alternating on a suitable serving dish.

note You can, of course, try just one of the cooking methods at a time if you prefer. Any of the three cooking methods works well with mussels as well as clams.

Steamed clams with ginger and garlic

This simple dish of steamed clams is flavoured with ginger, garlic and toasted sesame oil, and produces a wonderful aromatic broth.

serves 4

1kg cherrystone clams
2 garlic cloves, sliced
2.5cm piece of ginger, peeled and cut into thin strips
1 tablespoon grapeseed oil
1/2 tablespoon toasted sesame oil
1 leek, white part only, cut lengthways into long strips
250ml Dashi (see page 17)
soy sauce
freshly ground black pepper

1   Wash the clams thoroughly and place in a saucepan with the rest of ingredients except the soy sauce and pepper. Cover with a lid and cook over high heat for 10 minutes until the clams have opened.

2   Transfer the clams to a suitable dish, discarding any that have stayed closed. Add soy sauce and pepper to the cooking liquor to taste and then pour this over the top of the clams.

note   You can also use this method with mussels, and both make great dressings for noodles and pasta.

Slow-cooked salmon

Making this dish requires a little patience but the rewards are certainly well worth it. This sort of slow cooking produces salmon that looks almost raw, but does give it a very soft and delicate texture – and in the process also creates its own flavoursome cooking juices. To cook this dish in this way, you will

need a kitchen thermometer, to help keep the cooking temperature steady, and a plastic boiling bag in order to gain the best results.

serves 2

2 salmon fillets, each about 100g, skinned and boned
1 tablespoon sake
1 tablespoon light soy sauce
1 tablespoon Dashi (see page 17)
1cm piece of root ginger, peeled and finely shredded
30g butter
1 garlic clove, sliced

for the garnish
100g snow peas, shredded
olive oil for sautéing
salt and freshly ground black pepper
shiso cress (see page 253)

1 Bring a pan of water up to 65°C and maintain the temperature with the aid of a thermometer.

2 Place all the ingredients with the exception of the garnish items in a boiling bag. Immerse the bag in the water and, checking with the thermometer, maintain a temperature of 65°C for 12 minutes. Regulate the temperature by removing the pan from the heat if it becomes too hot and vice versa. Make sure no water enters the bag; it must remain completely waterproof.

3 Meanwhile, sauté the shredded snow peas for the garnish quickly in a little olive oil and season with salt and pepper, then arrange in the centre of a plate.

4 Remove the salmon carefully from the bag (it may be easier to pour it into a small dish first) and slice gently or leave whole if preferred, then place on top of the snow peas. Spoon a little of the juices from the bag around the salmon and garnish with shiso cress.

note It is important that the temperature remains at a constant 65°C during the cooking process to gain the maximum effect of the slow cooking.

Steamed scorpion fish

Steaming helps keep the purity and juiciness of the scorpion fish, while the ginger, garlic and sesame add a wonderful aroma to the flesh.

serves 4–6

1kg whole scorpion fish, cleaned, scaled and gutted
2 garlic cloves, thinly sliced
2 tablespoons finely shredded root ginger
4 cep mushrooms, cut in half
4 eringe mushrooms, cut in half
2 tablespoons sake
1/2 bunch of chives, finely chopped
3 tablespoons New-style oil (page 245)
3 tablespoons Sake soy (page 248)
French beans, blanched
1 summer truffle, thinly sliced
steamed rice to serve

1   Rinse the fish inside and out with cold water, pat dry with kitchen paper and place on a chopping board. On each side of fish, make parallel angled cuts about 2cm apart just through to the bone. This will enable the heat to penetrate and cook the fish evenly.

2   Place the fish on the plate on which you will serve it and spread the garlic and ginger across the length of the tail, then arrange the ceps and eringe mushrooms down one side. Pour over the sake and cook in a steamer for 12–15 minutes, until cooked – check with a knife at the thickest part to see if it is done.

3   When the fish is ready, sprinkle the chives over the tail and heat the New-style oil until just smoking. Pour the Sake soy over the fish and add the French beans and truffle slices. Finish by pouring the hot oil over the ginger, chives and garlic slices on the tail to sear and release the flavours.

4   Serve with bowls of steamed rice.

note   For more than 4 people use more than one fish, each fish should be no more than 1kg, unless you have a very large steamer. Ask your fishmonger to clean and scale the fish, leaving the head and fins intact. You can tell if the fish is fresh by the clearness of the eyes, the springiness of the flesh and the bright red colour of the gills.

Steamed John Dory with wild garlic leaves en papillote

When John Dory is filleted, each of the 2 fillets naturally splits into 3 pieces which, when folded in half, make perfect parcels for steaming. John Dory develops a beautifully silken texture when steamed, and the wild garlic leaves add a wonderful aroma that will surprise your guests when the parcels are opened at the table.

serves 6

1 large John Dory, skinned and filleted, then each fillet
* separated into 3 (see above)*
6 shiitake mushrooms, wiped and stalks removed
125g oyster mushrooms, wiped and stalks removed
12 asparagus spears, each cut at an angle into 3 pieces,
* then briefly blanched*
75g wild garlic leaves (ramsons or bear garlic), coarsely chopped
60g butter
sea salt and freshly ground black pepper
shichimi togarashi (see page 252)
6 tablespoons sake
6 tablespoons soy sauce

1   You will need a steamer big enough to cook the 6 parcels together. Preheat the oven to 150°C/gas 2. Cut out six 40cm diameter circles from baking parchment. Or do what we do in the restaurant kitchens, which is to take a piece of parchment bigger than the circle needed and fold it in half, then in half again at right angles to the first fold, and repeat this 3 times. Trim the open end of the folded parchment to the length of the radius of the required circle (20 cm). When you open the paper out, it will be an almost perfect circle.

2   Place a folded piece of fish neatly in the centre each of the parchment circles. Scatter one-sixth of the mushrooms, chopped asparagus and wild garlic leaves over each of the pieces of fish. Then place 10g of butter on top of each and season with salt, pepper and shichimi togarashi.

3   Fold each of the parchment rounds into a half-moon, taking care that the contents remain in the centre of the bag. Fold one of the corners up so it is at right angles to the flat side of the half-moon. Now fold over the rounded edge of the parcel with tight little folds, each one overlapping the next until you are two-thirds of the way round. Holding the last fold tightly, pick up the bag (making sure the sealed end is pointing downwards) and pour the sake and soy sauce into the opening. Fold up the last corner, again at right angles to the base, and continue making tight little folds around the top until you reach the end. Tuck the end round into the last corner and stand the parcel on its flat end (it should look like a Cornish pastie).

4   Place the parcels in the steamer and cook for 10–12 minutes, then remove them carefully and place them on a baking tray. Put in the preheated oven for 1 minute to dry the paper and allow the bags to puff up a little. Take care that the parchment doesn't burn while in the oven.

5   Serve immediately, cutting open the top of each parcel at the table.

notes   You can use this treatment with any fish, adjusting the cooking time according to the thickness of the fish. If wild garlic is not available try using spinach or celery leaves. For a really special treat, add a few truffle shavings to each parcel.

English spring vegetable medleys

This is the best way to appreciate these baby vegetables, as they are lightly steamed to retain a slight crunch and then tossed in a selection of appropriate dressings.

serves 4

1 small bunch of green French beans
1 small bunch of yellow French beans
4 baby carrots
4 baby turnips
4 baby beetroots
1/4 small pumpkin squash
4 red radishes
1 ripe fig, quartered
Matsuhisa dressing (see page 242)
Jalapeño dressing (see page 242)
Spicy lemon dressing (see page 242)

1   Trim the beans, carrots, turnips and beetroots, then trim and remove any seeds from the pumpkin.

2   Steam the vegetables separately; the cooking times will vary depending on their size and type. The beans will cook quickly, as will the pumpkin, then the carrots next, and finally the turnips and beetroots should take the longest. Check after 3 minutes to see how they are progressing, remembering that you need them to be slightly al dente.

3   When they are cooked, place them in bowls with the radishes and fig quarters, and dress with the sauces. Alternatively, place the vegetables together and keep the sauces separate, so your guests can choose their favourite to go with each different vegetable.

note   Try experimenting with different types of baby vegetables.

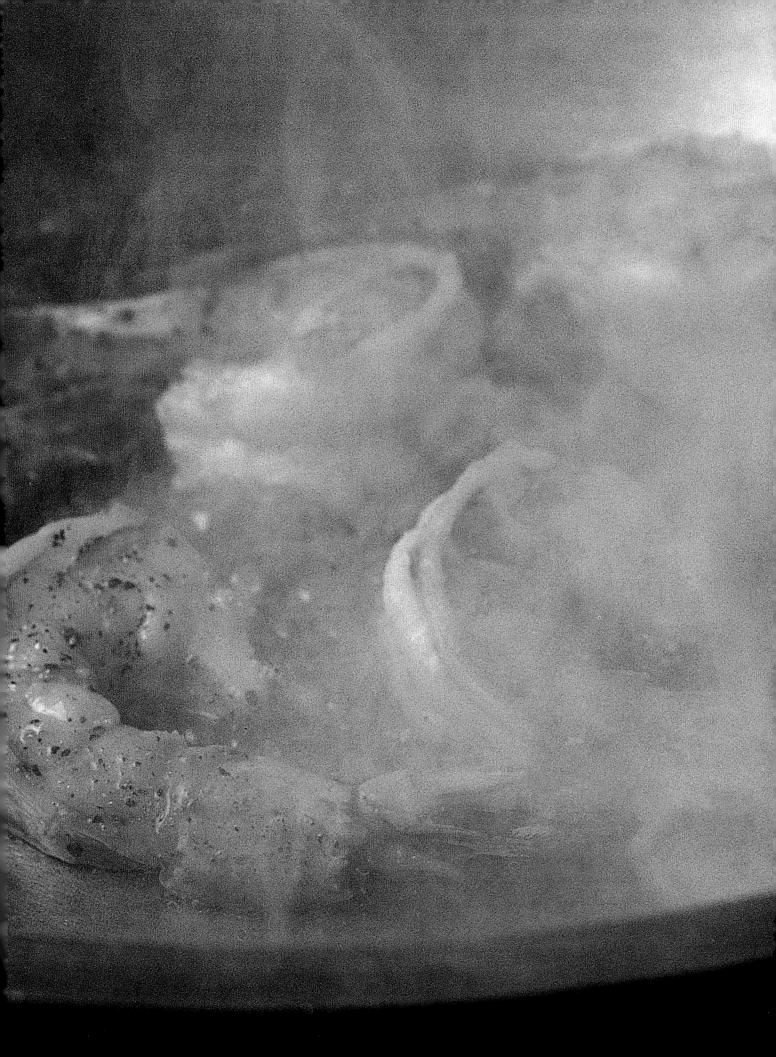

King crab with onion ginger salsa

Here king crab is quickly sautéed to retain its natural juices, then enhanced with Ginger Salsa. King crab legs are usually sold ready-cooked.

serves 2

2 cooked king crab legs
sea salt and freshly ground black pepper
1 tablespoon clarified butter (see page 126)
1 tablespoon plus 1 teaspoon sake
small handful of daikon radish sprouts (kaiware, see page 251)
4 tablespoons Ginger salsa (see page 243)

1   With a pair of scissors, cut away the shell around the crab legs (keeping the nicest pieces for decoration), leaving the meat in one piece. Remove any sinews from the end of the meat with a pair tweezers or small pliers.

2   Heat a frying pan over a medium heat and season the crab leg with salt and pepper. Add the clarified butter to the pan and quickly sauté the crab legs for 1–2 minutes on all sides.

3   Add the sake and allow almost all of it to evaporate, then add the daikon sprouts and allow to cook for 3 seconds only. Remove from the pan, together with the crab meat.

4   Place the crab legs on a suitable serving dish with the daikon sprouts alongside. Spoon the Ginger salsa over the crab legs and garnish with the pieces of crab shell.

note   Eating crab meat actually lowers the body's temperature and the ginger brings it back up, to balance out the effect. You can make this dish with cooked legs from ordinary crabs.

Baby octopus toban

The toban is a ceramic dish with a lid in which the food is cooked from the heat in the base and is then served sizzling at the table. The aromas that are released when the lid is removed are a wondrous delight. In this recipe, the flavour of the baby octopus is heightened with the saltiness of dried miso and the heat of the shichimi.

serves 2

12–16 (200g) baby octopus
1 tablespoon olive oil
2 tablespoons clarified butter (see page 126)
1 garlic clove, thinly sliced
8 okra, blanched
4 tablespoons sake
2 tablespoons yuzu juice (see page 253)
shichimi togarashi (see page 252)
2 teaspoons Dried miso (see page 249)

1   Cut out and remove the beak from each octopus, then push out the eyes from behind and cut them off. Turn the head inside out, remove all the innards and rinse thoroughly in running cold water. Rub the octopus in a bowl with salt to remove the slime and rinse off under cold water.

2   Preheat a grill and lightly grill the octopus on all sides for 1 minute.

3   Place the toban dish bases over a medium heat and allow to heat through. Working quickly, so as not to overcook the octopus, divide the olive oil and the clarified butter between the toban dishes, followed by the sliced garlic, octopus and okra, and allow to cook for a few seconds.

4   Pour in the sake, followed by the yuzu juice, then finish with a pinch of shichimi on top of each and the Dried miso.

5   Place the lid(s) on and serve while still sizzling.

note   When bringing this dish to the table, make sure that you sit it on a heatproof mat another heatproof dish as the heat from the ceramic bases can scorch the table. When removing the lid from a toban at the table, always use a heatproof cloth to prevent scalding.

Dover sole with spicy shiso ponzu

Dover sole is always a favourite in our London restaurants, and its delicate but firm flesh is perfectly matched by this tangy dressing.

serves 2

vegetable oil, for deep-frying
1 Dover sole, about 400g, filleted and skinned (but backbone reserved and head removed)
sea salt and freshly ground black pepper
flour for dusting
2 tablespoons olive oil
1 tablespoon clarified butter (see page 126)
4 tablespoons Shiso ponzu (see page 244)
whole shiitake mushrooms to garnish (optional)

1 Heat a medium-to-large pan of oil (8–10cm deep) to a temperature of 180°C. Using a pair of chopsticks, hold the tail of the sole bone and carefully lower it into the hot oil. Allow to cook for 2–3 minutes until it is completely crisp. Again using chopsticks, remove it from the oil, place one end on a clean flat surface and bend the bone into a 'U 'shape (this will be possible only while it is still hot). Allow to drain on kitchen paper.

2 Season the sole fillets with salt and pepper, and lightly dust in flour, shaking off any excess. Heat a large non-stick frying pan over medium heat and add the olive oil and clarified butter. Place the fillets into the pan, skin side down, and gently sauté for 2 minutes, then turn them over and cook for another 1–2 minutes.

3 Carefully remove from the pan and place the fillets side by side on a serving dish. Spoon the Shiso ponzu around them and place the fried bone over the top. Garnish with some shiitake mushrooms if you like.

note The crispy fried bone can be eaten as well. Lemon sole and plaice are good substitutes if Dover sole is not available.

Monkfish with fennel salad

Monkfish and fennel is a classic combination in Western cooking, but here we have given it a Japanese twist, with the addition of a tangy hot-and-sour dressing.

serves 2

5 baby fennel bulbs
sea salt and freshly ground black pepper
2 tablespoons fresh orange juice
2 tablespoons olive oil
150g skinless boneless monkfish fillet
flour for dusting
6 baby plum tomatoes
small quantity of Spicy sour sauce (see page 246)

1 Thinly slice the baby fennel on a mandolin grater and place the slices in a non-reactive bowl. Season with salt and pepper, add the orange juice and olive oil, and toss well.

2 Slice the monkfish across into medallions about 1cm thick. Pat these dry with kitchen paper and season with salt and pepper.

3 Heat some olive oil in a non-stick frying pan over high heat. Dust the monkfish with flour and shake off any excess. Cook the fish medallions for 2 minutes on each side and drain on a metal rack.

4 Drain off any excess liquid from the baby fennel and place a neat pile on a serving dish. Arrange the monkfish around the fennel and decorate with the baby plum tomatoes and a little Spicy sour sauce.

note Monkfish has a high water content, so the flour helps to form a seal around the flesh during cooking.

Crispy Gloucester Old Spot pork belly with spicy miso

Succulent crispy pork belly is here combined with ginger, garlic and Spicy Miso – and its hint of toasted sesame oil. Gloucester Old Spot is a traditional rare breed of pig from the apple orchards of Gloucestershire, distinguished by its large floppy ears and black spots on its back, as well as the succulence and fine full flavour of its meat. Ancient folklore claims that the spots are bruises caused by apples falling on the pigs as they foraged in the orchards for food.

serves4

500g Gloucester Old Spot pork belly, bones removed
2 red chillies. split in half lengthways
100g root ginger, peeled and sliced
4 garlic cloves, sliced
sea salt and freshly ground black pepper

for the garnish
6 tablespoons Spicy miso (see page 245)
1 tablespoon finely diced red chilli, deseeded
1 tablespoon finely chopped chives or spring onion
1 tablespoon finely diced red onion

1 Using a very sharp knife, carefully remove the skin from the pork belly, keeping as much fat as possible attached to the belly meat.

2 Place the belly in a flat, shallow heavy-based pan just large enough for it to sit snugly on the bottom. Add the chillies, ginger and garlic, and season with salt and pepper. Add just enough water to cover the belly and place a plate on top to keep the belly submersed in the liquid, then cover with the lid.

3 Place over high heat and bring to the boil, then reduce the heat to a bare simmer and cook for 1 hour (check from time to time that the pork belly is always immersed in the stock, and top up with more water if necessary). Remove from the heat and allow the belly to cool in the stock, then refrigerate overnight.

4 Remove the pork belly from the stock, drain and pat dry with kitchen paper. Then cut it into strips about 2cm wide.

5 Place a dry non-stick frying pan over high heat and fry the pork belly strips on all sides until uniformly golden brown and crisp, adjusting the heat where necessary during cooking. Drain on kitchen paper.

6 While the meat is still hot, place the strips on a clean chopping board and cut into bite-sized cubes.

7 Spoon half the Spicy miso on the bottom of a suitable serving dish and arrange the pork belly pieces on top of the sauce. Spoon the remaining sauce over the top of the belly. Mix the finely chopped chilli, chives and red onion together and sprinkle on the top of each piece of pork.

note You can, of course, use pork belly from any breed of pig for this dish.

Lamb marinated in miso

Lamb is rarely used in Japanese cooking, but in this recipe the miso marinade transforms the lamb into something quite different and truly delicious.

serves 3

sea salt and freshly ground black pepper
handful of dried gourd shavings (kanpyo, see page 251)
1 whole rack of lamb, French trimmed (6 chops, see left)
Spicy miso (see page 245)
a little olive oil
3 white asparagus spears
3 heads of baby bok choy
3 garlic shoots (see page 250)
3 tablespoons Spicy lemon dressing (see page 242)

1   At least 6 hours ahead, bring a pan of water to the boil. Rub salt into the gourd shavings, rinse with cold water and plunge into the boiling water for 2 minutes. Drain well.

2   Trim off any excess fat from the lamb and wrap the exposed bones with the dried gourd. Place the rack meat in the Spicy miso, making sure the wrapped bones stick out clear of the liquid. Leave to marinate for 6 hours.

3   Preheat the oven to 200°C/gas 6 and preheat a grill or barbecue. Heat an ovenproof frying pan with some olive oil in it. Remove the lamb from the marinade and quickly brown it all over in the oil over high heat for 2 minutes, then transfer to the oven for 12 minutes to finish cooking (2–3 minutes longer, if you prefer it medium to well done).

4   Meanwhile, bring another pan of water to the boil. Brush the asparagus stalks with olive oil and season with salt and pepper. Cook under the grill or on the barbecue until just tender. Blanch the bok choy quickly in the boiling salted water for 1 minute and the garlic shoots for 30 seconds, then drain.

5   Remove the lamb from the oven and transfer to a warm plate to rest for 2 minutes. Then cut into 6 chops and arrange on a serving dish. Place the grilled asparagus, bok choy and garlic shoots neatly around the lamb and dress with the Spicy lemon dressing. Wrapping the bones with the dried gourd, as well as giving a Japanese look, allows your guests to pick up the chops with their fingers.

Roast duck breast with orange miso

Orange miso is the perfect accompaniment to this quick and simple duck dish.

serves 2

5 tablespoons Den miso (see page 244)
5 tablespoons fresh orange juice, the grated zest from 2 oranges
  and 1 whole orange, cut in half and the flesh scooped out
150–200g duck breast
olive oil
50g sugar snap peas
50g chanterelle mushrooms
sea salt and freshly ground black pepper
2 bamboo or banana leaves

1   About 2 hours ahead, mix the Den Miso, orange juice and orange zest together in a non-reactive bowl and set 2 tablespoons aside. Trim off any excess fat from the duck breast and score the remaining fat with a sharp knife, then cut it into 2 even pieces. Put the duck breast into the bowl of orange miso and leave to marinate for 2 hours.

2   Towards the end of that time, preheat the oven to 200°C/gas 6. Heat some olive oil in an ovenproof frying pan over high heat. Drain any excess miso from the duck breasts and place them, skin side down, into the frying pan. Cook for 2 minutes, then turn over and place in the oven for a further 8 minutes to finish cooking.

3   Season the sugar snap peas and mushrooms with sea salt and pepper; place a frying pan over medium heat and quickly sauté in olive oil for 2 minutes, then drain.

4   Toast the bamboo or banana leaves over an open flame and place in the empty orange cases. Place the duck breasts inside the leaf-lined orange and drizzle over the reserved orange miso. Decorate with the mushrooms and peas, and place on a suitable serving dish.

note   Cooking the duck breast fat side down helps to release excess fat from the skin and make it crisp.

Shabu shabu with Iberian pork

Shabu shabu means 'swish, swish', the sound created by the thinly sliced meat being moved from side to side in the pot. It is said that this dish originated around the thirteenth century, as a way for Genghis Khan to feed his Mongolian army. The idea was that they would all gather round a boiling pot and dip thinly sliced meat in it, hence the quick cooking time to save precious fuel. It arrived in Japan in the twentieth century and is a national favourite. Now popular all over Asia, it is fast becoming popular in the West. Although this is an unusual technique and obviously not really sautéing, we've decided that it fits best here in this chapter.

serves 4

200g fresh pork loin, preferably from Iberian black pigs
2 bunches of watercress
2 bunches of enoki mushrooms, trimmed
8 Chinese cabbage or Napa cabbage leaves
8 shiitake mushrooms, stalks removed
100g Inaniwa noodles or tagliatelle
salt
180ml Jalapeño ponzu (see page 245)
13cm square piece of konbu (see page 251)

1   Trim off the outside fat and any sinew from the pork loin and place it in the freezer for 20 minutes (this gets it really cold and firm, so it can be sliced more easily).

2   On a large serving platter, arrange the watercress, enoki mushrooms, cabbage leaves and shiitake mushrooms neatly in the centre of the dish.

3   Cut the pork loin into as near wafer-thin slices as possible and fold each slice in half. Arrange these overlapping around the edge of the serving platter, then cover and refrigerate until ready for serving.

4   Cook the noodles in boiling salted water, refresh with cold water and drain. Place on a separate serving dish in 4 separate neat piles. Put the Jalapeño Ponzu in 4 separate dipping bowls.

5   When ready to cook, place a portable gas stove on a table and put a shabu shabu pot or heatproof ceramic dish or shallow saucepan half-filled with water on top. Place the konbu in the water and bring to the boil. Once it has boiled, turn the heat down to a gentle simmer and remove the konbu.

6   Place the platter of pork and vegetables on the table, together with the noodles and the 4 dipping bowls of Jalapeño Ponzu.

7   To eat, pick up a piece of pork with your chopsticks, dip it into the boiling stock and swish from side to side for 10 seconds, then dip it in the Jalapeño ponzu and eat. Continue in this way, also cooking the pork, mushrooms and vegetables of your choice (the vegetables will need to be left in the stock a little longer to cook) until the whole platter has been consumed.

8   Finally, place the noodles in the hot stock and eat these last.

note   You can use any pork or beef for this dish, as well as scallops, prawns and fish, just as long as the pieces are small enough to cook quickly in the stock.

Sukiyaki Nobu-style

Sukiyaki is very popular in Japan and normally eaten in the winter months. It is a great meal to share family style, where everybody sits around the table watching it cook. In Japan, the poached eggs are served raw in dipping cups and the beef is dipped into the raw egg before eating. Don't over-boil the sauce, as it will be too strong; have a little hot water on hand, in case this happens.

serves 4

200g kobe or wagyu beef or well-marbled rib or sirloin of beef
100g onions, sliced
1 bunch of watercress
1 bunch of enoki mushrooms
100g inaniwa noodles or tagliatelle
4 soft-poached eggs

for the sauce

3 tablespoons soy sauce

3 tablespoons mirin (Japanese rice wine, see page 252)

3 tablespoons sake

Dashi (see page 17) or beef stock

3 tablespoons sugar

1   About half an hour before, make the sauce by mixing all the ingredients in a saucepan and warming gently until all the sugar has dissolved.

2   Trim off the outside fat and any sinew from the beef and place it in the freezer for 20 minutes (this gets it really cold and firm, so it can be sliced easily). Slice the beef as near to wafer-thin as possible, and fold each slice in half.

3   Place the sliced onions in the bottom of a sukiyaki pan or similar shallow saucepan. Arrange the beef slices on the top of those, with the watercress and enoki mushrooms in the centre.

4   Cook the noodles in boiling salted water, refresh with cold water and drain. Place on a separate serving dish in 4 separate neat piles. Place each of the 4 poached eggs in each of 4 separate dipping bowls.

5   When ready to cook, place a portable gas stove on a table and put the sukiyaki pan or heatproof ceramic dish or shallow saucepan on top. Turn on the gas and pour enough of the sauce to come up to the underside of the beef. Bring to the boil and then turn down a simmer, stirring occasionally and adding more sauce if needed. When the beef is just cooked, turn off the gas and eat by dipping the beef and the onions into the soft poached egg in the dipping cup.

6   When all the meat has been eaten, turn on the gas again and place the noodles into the hot sauce (add more sauce if needed) and heat through and eat these last.

grill

Atlantic cod, halibut and salmon with saikyo miso

The Pacific black cod, or sablefish, with miso has become perhaps one of the most famous dishes at all of the Nobu restaurants. Here we use the same technique and cooking method with Atlantic cod, halibut and salmon. Some of our customers like to squeeze fresh lemon juice over the top to balance out the sweetness of the Saikyo miso, but this is a matter of personal taste.

serves 2

2 cod, halibut or salmon fillets, each about 125g, still with the
  skin but any pin bones removed

for the Saikyo miso
100ml sake
100ml mirin (Japanese rice wine, see page 252)
150g caster sugar
300g white miso paste (see page 253)

for the garnish
cherry plum tomatoes on the vine
small slender courgettes, ideally with their flowers attached,
  briefly blanched and refreshed

1   About 2 days ahead, make the Saikyo miso: in heavy-
based non-reactive saucepan, bring the sake and mirin to
the boil, and continue to boil for 2–3 minutes to allow the
alcohol to evaporate.

2   Using a wooden spoon, stir in the sugar until it has
dissolved, then slowly mix in the miso paste, a little at a
time. Cook over medium heat, stirring constantly so as
not to let the mixture burn, for 10–15 minutes.

3   Strain the mixture through a sieve to remove any
lumps, allow to cool and then chill until quite cold.

4   Place the fish in a non-reactive container, pour a good
splash of the Saikyo miso over each fillet and leave to
marinate for 1–2 days in the refrigerator.

5   When you want to cook the fish, preheat a hot grill or
the oven to 200°C/gas 6. Place the fillets in the grill pan
or on a non-stick baking sheet and cook under the grill or
in the preheated oven for 10–12 minutes, turning once if
grilling, until cooked through and golden on the outside.

6   Place on a serving dish and dress the plate with a
little extra Saikyo miso and some cherry plum tomatoes
on the vine or small slender courgettes.

Grilled sea trout with fried spinach

Crunchy spinach tempura makes a prefect foil for grilled sea trout enhanced with a spicy vinegar-based sauce.

serves 4

vegetable oil for deep-frying
4 sea trout fillets, each about 150g
sea salt and freshly ground black pepper
32 baby spinach leaves, well dried
flour for dusting
1 recipe quantity of Tempura batter (see page 99)

for the Spicy-sour sauce
1 tablespoon clarified butter (see page 126)
$1/2$ teaspoon chilli garlic sauce (see page 250)
150ml Dashi (see page 17)
2 tablespoons light soy sauce
2 tablespoons sake
$1/2$ teaspoon freshly ground black pepper
2 tablespoons rice vinegar
a little kuzu or cornflour mixed with water

1   Preheat a barbecue, grill or griddle pan and heat oil for deep-frying to 180°C.

2   Lightly rub the trout fillets with and season with salt and pepper, then cook on the barbecue, grill or griddle pan for 5–6 minutes until just cooked through.

3   While the trout is cooking, dust the spinach leaves in flour and carefully dip one side only of each leaf in the tempura batter and cook in small batches, draining them on kitchen paper.

4   Make the sauce by gently heating the clarified butter, then add the Chilli garlic sauce and cook for a few seconds. Add the Dashi and bring to the boil. Add the soy sauce, sake and pepper, then finish with the rice vinegar and bring back just to the boil. Thicken slightly with the kuzu or cornflour mixture and remove from the heat.

5   To serve, divide the spinach leaves between 4 plates, arranging them like the petals of a flower. Put a trout fillet next to them and spoon a little of the sauce around the fish.

note   As there is more than one cooking process involved in this dish and the timing is crucial to keep the spinach tempura crisp, it may be easier for two people to help in its preparation.

Mackerel shio-yaki and vegetable salad

This is a very simple way with mackerel – the succulent flesh is enhanced by the crunchiness of the vegetables and the sherry vinegar dressing. Shio-yaki is a traditional Japanese method of cooking fish, poultry or meat that involves salting and grilling.

serves 2

1 red pepper
1/4 cucumber
1 yellow courgette
3 large Chinese cabbage leaves
2 boneless skin-on mackerel fillets
sea salt and freshly ground black pepper
4 tablespoons olive oil
2 tablespoons sherry vinegar

1   Cut the pepper in half and remove the stalk and the seeds, then cut the flesh into 5mm dice and place in a mixing bowl. Cut the cucumber in half and remove the seeds with a spoon, then cut into 5mm dice and add to the mixing bowl. Top and tail the yellow courgette and cut lengthways into 5mm thick strips, then into 5mm dice. Add to the bowl. Lay the cabbage leaves flat on top of one another and cut into 5mm strips, then into 5mm dice. Add to the bowl.

2   Preheat a barbecue, grill or griddle pan and the oven to 180°C/gas 4. Season the mackerel fillets with salt and pepper, and brush with a little of the olive oil. Place the fillets, skin side to the heat, on the barbecue, grill or griddle pan and cook for 1 minute on each side. Transfer to an ovenproof dish and cook in the oven for a further 6 minutes.

3   Add the sherry vinegar and remaining olive oil to the diced vegetables and toss together. Season with salt and pepper to taste, then put on a serving dish and top with the cooked mackerel fillets.

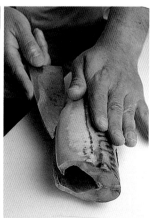

Toro steak with teriyaki balsamic sauce

You will probably be amazed at quite how sweet and subtly flavoured roasted garlic can be, and here it makes the perfect accompaniment to lightly seared toro (tuna belly) steak.

serves 2

1 whole head of garlic
2 toro (tuna belly) fillets, each about 100g
sea salt and freshly ground black pepper
Balsamic teriyaki sauce (see page 247), warmed through
handful of baby shiso leaves (see page 253)
handful of daikon cress (kaiware, see page 251)

1   Preheat the oven to 180°C/gas 4. Trim the root and the head of the garlic and remove any loose outside skin but still keep the head intact. Wrap in foil, place in an earthenware dish and roast for 20 minutes.

2   While that is cooking, preheat a barbecue, grill or griddle pan. Season the tuna fillets with salt and pepper and briefly sear each of them on all the sides for 2–3 minutes, keeping the centre rare.

3   To serve, spoon a little of the hot Balsamic teriyaki sauce on each of 2 plates, cut each tuna steak and the roasted garlic in half. Place the tuna steak halves in the middle of each plate and garnish with the shiso leaves and daikon cress, and a roasted garlic half.

Grilled venison with salted plum and wasabi

Here fiery wasabi and salted plums are brought together to marry with grilled venison. In Japan, wasabi and salted plum is a favourite combination and it makes a perfect accompaniment for this dish.

serves 2

4 baby beetroots, trimmed
4 venison loin steaks, each about 75g
sea salt and freshly ground black pepper
olive oil for brushing
4 fresh cep mushrooms, halved
1 bunch of watercress, stalks removed

for the Wasabi Pepper Sauce
1 1/2 teaspoons wasabi powder (see page 253)
1 tablespoon water
2 1/2 teaspoons soy sauce
2 1/2 teaspoons light soy sauce
3 tablespoons plus 1 teaspoon Dashi (see page 17)
1 teaspoon freshly ground black pepper

for the Wasabi Plum Sauce
8 whole umeboshi (Japanese salted plums, see page 253)
1 tablespoon clarified butter (see page 126)
1/2 garlic clove, thinly sliced
2 tablespoons sake
100ml Wasabi Pepper Sauce (above)

1   Preheat a barbecue, grill or griddle pan. Blanch the baby beetroots in boiling salted; they should still be al dente. Using some kitchen paper, wipe the outside skin off the beetroots, then cut them into halves or quarters, depending on their size (you may need to wear rubber gloves to prevent staining to your hands).

2   Season the venison fillets with salt and pepper, and brush with a little olive oil.

3   Make the Wasabi Pepper Sauce: put the wasabi powder in a bowl and mix with the water. Cover with clingfilm and leave to stand for 10 minutes to allow the flavour to develop. Add the other ingredients and mix well.

4   Make the Wasabi Plum Sauce: keeping 2 of the umeboshi separate for garnish, remove the stones from the other 6 and roughly chop them. Place a frying pan over medium heat, then add the clarified butter and garlic. When the aroma of the garlic is released, add the chopped umeboshi and cook for a further minute, keeping the temperature low so as not to brown the garlic. Add the sake, bring to the boil, then add the Wasabi pepper sauce and bring back to the boil. Remove from the heat immediately (or the wasabi will lose its pungency), season with salt and pepper, and keep warm.

5   Place the venison fillets on the barbecue, grill or griddle pan and cook for 2–3 minutes on each side, depending on their thickness (they need to be still pink in the centre).

6   At the same time, season the mushroom halves and the blanched baby beetroots with salt and pepper, then barbecue, grill or griddle for 2–3 minutes until cooked.

7   Arrange the venison, ceps and beetroot on 2 plates, spoon a little of the Wasabi plum sauce around and garnish with watercress and the whole umeboshi.

note   Although everybody seems to refer to umeboshi as a Japanese salted plum, it is, in fact, a salted apricot.

rice, sushi and noodles

Nobu style paella

In this recipe you can use any selection of your favourite fish or shellfish. We sometimes make this dish for the staff when we have assortment of fish trimmings at the end of the day.

serves 4–6

large pinch of saffron threads
700 ml Japanese rice
4–6 baby octopus
4–6 small squid
4–6 shelled scallops
4–6 Mediterranean prawns in the shell
4–6 langoustines in the shell
4–6 clams in the shell
380ml Dashi (see page 17)
sea salt and freshly ground black pepper
8–12 morel mushrooms
4–6 fresh cep mushrooms
100g podded fresh green peas
100g fresh broad beans, podded and skinned

1   Lightly toast the saffron threads under a grill or salamander for a few seconds until they become slightly darker (this enables them to impart more colour and flavour to the rice).

2   Rinse the rice and leave it in cold water to soak for a while, then drain.

3   Prepare the seafood, scrubbing shells, removing beards, etc., and discard any shells that stay open when tapped.

4   Place the rice, saffron, Dashi, salt and pepper in a heatproof heavy earthenware pot that has a tight-fitting lid. Add the rest of the ingredients, then place the lid on top and set over high heat. Turn the heat down to medium just before it boils and cook for 10 minutes, then turn down the temperature to very low and cook for a further 10 minutes.

5   Finally, turn up the heat to full for 30 seconds, then remove from the heat and let the paella rest for 10 minutes before serving.

note   A wonderful addition to this dish is a little sprinkling of bonito flakes (see page 250) on the top when serving, as this gives it a slightly smoky flavour.

Parmesan rice

This dish is quite simple to make but very rewarding, as it has the wonderful heady aroma of white truffle and is full of umami flavour.

serves 4

700ml Japanese rice
380ml Dashi (see page 17)
120g freshly grated Parmesan cheese
thinly sliced white truffle, to serve

1   Rinse the rice well in cold water and leave to soak in fresh cold water for 20 minutes, then drain.

2   Put the rice, Dashi and Parmesan into a heatproof earthenware dish with a tight-fitting lid, mix them together well and place the lid on top. Set the dish over a high heat, turn the heat down to medium just as it comes to the boil and cook for 15 minutes, then turn the heat down to low and cook for a further 10 minutes, making sure that the lid is not taken off during the cooking process.

3   Remove from the heat and allow to stand for 5 minutes with the lid still on.

4   Just before serving, remove the lid from the dish and slice the white truffle thinly over the top of the rice. Scoop the rice into bowls at the table.

note   For the best results, make sure that you use good-quality Parmesan and that you grate it just before you mix it into the rice.

Rice pizza

This Nobu version of pizza makes ideal finger food or can even be served as a light lunch. The amounts given here make three pizza bases, but you can store / freeze the other two bases for another day. With this dish there are countless combinations for the toppings or you could just stick to one type.

The dough for the base is very elastic and must be well rested, or it will shrink during cooking.

Be sure to serve the pizza fairly quickly after making it, so the base does not get the chance to become too soggy from the liquid in the toppings.

Mochi flour is milled from mochi rice, a short-grained, glutinous rice. It is used to thicken sauces, as well as for breading foods for frying and for making traditional desserts and bakes, or rice dumplings known as Japanese *mochi*.

makes 3 small pizza bases and toppings for 1

for the bases

150g mochi flour (glutinous rice flour, see page 252), plus more
   for dusting
pinch of salt
1 tablespoon olive oil, plus more for cooking
320ml boiling water

for the toppings

2 teaspoons salmon eggs
2 teaspoons caviar
1 slice (10g) of smoked salmon
1 slice (10g) of cooked lobster
1 slice (10g) of pickled herring
1 slice (10g) of cooked crab claw

for the garnish

finely shredded daikon
shiso leaves (see page 253)
coriander leaves
chervil leaves
bonito flakes (see page 250)

1   Put the mochi flour, salt and olive oil into the bowl of a food processor. Turn it on, pour in the boiling water and mix to a smooth dough. Turn out on a floured board and leave to rest for 1 hour.

2   Divide the dough into 3 (there is enough to make 3 bases) and roll one piece out as thinly as possible into a circle. Allow to rest in the refrigerator for 20 minutes. Store or freeze the other bases for another time.

3   Heat a non-stick frying pan over a medium heat, add ¹/₂ tablespoon of olive oil and fry the base in the pan until light and golden, turning it frequently and adjusting the temperature to prevent burning, for 2–3 minutes. When cooked, turn out on a clean chopping board and allow to cool, then cut into 6 equal wedges.

4   Place each of the 6 different toppings on to one of each of the 6 wedges and place the shredded daikon in the middle. Decorate each slice with the garnish of your choice and serve.

Sushi rice (shari)

Getting your sushi rice right is a crucial element in successful sushi-making. The preparation of the rice is so important that most sushi establishments in Japan have chefs whose sole responsibility is to cook the rice. One secret is always to measure your ingredients very carefully.

makes 5 cups

720g Japanese short-grain rice
900ml cold water

for the Sushi vinegar (Shari Zu)
200ml Red Japanese Vinegar (regular Japanese rice vinegar will do)
2 tablespoons plus 2 teaspoons sea salt
1 tablespoon mirin (Japanese rice wine, see page 252)
145ml caster sugar
about 4 cm square piece of konbu (see page 251)

1   First, make the Sushi Vinegar (this can be made well in advance and will keep in the fridge for up to a month). In a non-reactive saucepan, gently heat 150ml of the vinegar with the salt, mirin and sugar until the sugar has completely dissolved – but do not let the liquid boil! Wipe the konbu with a clean damp cloth to remove any residue and add to the liquid. Remove from the heat and allow to cool completely. When cold, add the remaining vinegar. This quantity will be enough to make two batches of sushi rice.

2   In a large bowl of cold water, wash the rice, rubbing it and rinsing it frequently with fresh water until all the excess starch has gone and the water stops being cloudy and is clear. Soak in fresh cold water for about 30 minutes and then drain in a sieve.

3   To a heavy-based saucepan, add the rice and the 900ml of water. Bring to the boil over a high heat for 1 minute, then reduce the heat to low for and continue cooking for a further 5 minutes. Lastly, return the heat to high for 10 seconds, then remove the pan from the heat. Allow to sit for 15 minutes, then drain off any excess water.

4   Transfer the hot rice to a wooden Japanese rice tub or wide shallow container and spread out thinly with a rice paddle or wide wooden spoon. Sprinkle half the sushi vinegar (about 150ml) over the rice and, working quickly with the rice paddle in a slicing motion across the rice, cut through the rice from the bottom of the tub so that it gets turned over and blends in the vinegar. Be careful not to squash or over-stir the rice, as this will make it become too sticky. Cover with a clean wet cloth and use while at room temperature within 1 hour. Do not allow it to become too cold or hard.

note   During the summer the rice will need less soaking, around 15 minutes.

Nigiri sushi European-style

Professional sushi chefs train for years to perfect their technique, but although sushi made at home will never be on a par with that of a professional sushi chef, this is no reason not to try making it. The act of making it yourself will give you a great sense of accomplishment and is very rewarding – and lots of fun in the process. The more you practise, the better your understanding will be.

The easiest way to start is to stick to one type of fish until you get the hang of it and then progress on to different types of fish. The two most important things to remember when making sushi are, first, that you buy only the freshest of fish (it should be no more than a day old) and, second, it should be eaten straight away, as soon as it's made; never put it in the fridge for later. You should, of course, ensure that your hands, chopping board and utensils are scrupulously clean.

When eating sushi you should have the barest minimum of soy sauce in you dipping bowl so as not to swamp the sushi in it, and the fish side should be dipped into the soy sauce, not the rice, otherwise the rice will disintegrate and ends up in the dipping bowl. There is no need to mix wasabi into the soy sauce, as it has already been added when the sushi was being made.

There are numerous combinations of sushi ingredients, from raw and cooked fish and shellfish to meat and vegetables. The following list is by no means exhaustive but is here as a basic guide:

tuna, sea bass, turbot, snapper, sea bream, flounder, shelled cooked prawns, salmon, salmon eggs, caviar, smoked fish such as salmon, eel or mackerel, cured fish such as gravlax or pickled herring, squid, scallops, cooked lobster, cooked crab, sea urchin, seared foie gras, seared wagyu beef, grilled mushrooms.

serves 4 (about 24 nigiri sushi pieces)

2 cups of Sushi rice (see page 194)
about 400g skinned fish fillet or other topping
1 tablespoon wasabi
sushi gari (pickled ginger), to serve
soy sauce, for dipping

for the hand vinegar (tezu)
3 tablespoons water
1 tablespoon rice vinegar

1   On a clean cutting board, place the fish fillet horizontally with the skin side up and the tail on the side of the preferred hand. Hold the knife in your preferred hand so that the top is inclined away from the fish, and from the other side of the fillet start cutting thin slices (about 5mm thick), keeping the blade at an acute angle to achieve a clean cut across the grain. You can apply pressure with your non-preferred hand to the outside of the fish to keep it firm, but care must be taken that you do not cut yourself. The fish is sliced in one drawing stroke, letting the weight of the knife do the work as you draw back the blade. Once all the fish has been sliced, cover with a clean damp cloth.

2   Mix the ingredients for the hand vinegar together and place in a small bowl.

3   To make the nigiri sushi, dip your fingers into the hand vinegar and rub your palms together. This will help stop the rice sticking to your hands. You should have a light covering of the hand vinegar – be careful, if you have too much, it will prevent the rice sticking together.

4   Pick a little more than a tablespoon of rice with your preferred hand and shape it into a rectangle (about 4x2cm). Place the rice across the insides of the first joint of the fingers of your preferred hand and, with the index and middle fingers of your other hand, press the rice into a firmer rectangle shape (the pressure should be firm but gentle, so as not to mash the rice), then turn the rice over to apply equal pressure to the other side.

5   Pick up a slice of fish with the non-preferred hand and place it across the first joints of the fingers in that hand, then smear a tiny amount of wasabi across the length of the slice, using the index finger of the preferred hand (while still holding the rice rectangle in the palm of that hand).

6   Place the rectangle of rice on top of the fish and press the rice and fish firmly together with the index and middle fingers of the preferred hand, then turn the sushi over to apply equal pressure to the other side.

7   Arrange the sushi on a serving dish and serve with pickled ginger and small dishes of soy sauce.

Bo sushi with herring

Bo sushi, also known as loaf or stick sushi, is an easier way to make sushi. The fish (or shellfish or vegetables) is placed on a sheet of konbu or nori seaweed and rolled around the rice. The finished rolls can be made a couple of hours in advance and then cut into pieces for eating.

serves 4

sea salt

4 fresh herrings, filleted

4 pieces of shiraita konbu (white konbu, see page 251)

16 caper berries

4 cups of Sushi rice (see page 194)

4 teaspoons toasted sesame seeds

pickled ginger (gari, see page 250) for garnish

soy sauce for dipping

bamboo or banana leaves for serving

for the marinade for the herring

150ml rice vinegar

5 tablespoons water

1 tablespoon caster sugar

1 tablespoon light soy sauce

for the marinade for the konbu

6 tablespoons water

6 tablespoons rice vinegar

1 tablespoon light soy sauce

1   Sprinkle a little sea salt on both sides of the herring fillets and leave them to stand for 30 minutes.

2   Wash off the salt and pat the fillets dry. Mix all the ingredients for the herring marinade together and immerse the fillets in the marinade. Leave to stand for 10 minutes, then drain and pat dry.

3   Place the konbu marinade ingredients in a flat, wide pan and add the sheets of konbu. Simmer very gently over a low heat for 20 minutes until they have become soft and translucent. Leave to cool in the liquid, then trim each sheet to the same size as the herring fillets.

4   Remove the stalks from 8 caper berries and roughly chop them, then fold into the sushi rice, along with the toasted sesame seeds.

5   To assemble, place a large sheet of cling film on a chopping board and lay a sheet of konbu horizontally in the centre. Place a herring fillet on top of the konbu, skin side down, and then arrange 1 cup of sushi rice along the length of the fillet. Wrap the end of the clingfilm nearest you over the top of the rice and roll the loaf up. Grabbing the ends of the clingfilm, keep rolling the loaf on the surface of the chopping board so the contents inside the clingfilm become tight and firm, resembling a sausage shape. Repeat the whole process for the remaining konbu and herring fillets.

6   When ready to serve, remove the clingfilm from the loaves and place them on a clean chopping board. With a sharp knife, cut each loaf across into slices about 2cm thick and arrange on a suitable serving dish atop bamboo or banana leaves. Garnish with the remaining caper berries and pickled ginger, and serve soy sauce separately for dipping.

note   This dish can also be made using mackerel, but you will need to salt the mackerel for 1 hour and peel off the skin after marinating.

Freshwater eel and white truffle egg roll

The sweetness of the eel and the delicacy of the sushi omelette, combined with white truffle, make this a very special dish. Unagi kabayaki, ready-grilled freshwater eel, is very popular in Japan and readily available at Japanese food stores. When opening the packs of eel, do reserve the tasty juices, which we spoon on to the plate under the rolls.

serves 2

4 large eggs
4 tablespoons Dashi (see page 17)
1 1/2 tablespoons sugar
1 teaspoon salt
1 teaspoon soy sauce
100g grilled freshwater eel (unagi kabayaki, see above)
olive oil, for frying
a little sliced white truffle

1 In a non-reactive bowl, beat together the eggs, dashi, sugar, salt and soy sauce, then strain through a fine sieve.

2 Preheat a salamander or grill. Chop the eel into chunks and grill for 1–2 minutes to warm through.

3 Place a well-oiled square Japanese omelette pan (*tamago*) over a low heat and pour in about a quarter of the egg, then spread it evenly by tilting, as if making a crêpe. As it bubbles and begins to cook and set, roll it up towards the back of the pan (away from you) and oil the pan again with kitchen paper dipped in olive oil.

4 Pour in another quarter of the egg, ensuring it goes underneath the first roll, and cook in the same way as the first. Roll the first omelette at the back of the pan over the top of the second towards the front of the pan and then push the whole roll to the back. Oil the pan again and repeat until all the egg has been used up. When cooking the last omelette, add the eel and truffle to the back end and roll everything up again to the front of the pan.

5 Turn the roll out on to a bamboo sushi mat and roll up in the mat like a sushi roll, squeezing out any excess juices, and leave to cool.

6 When cool, slice the roll into rounds about 1.5cm thick and serve on a suitable dish.

note The temperature of the pan is crucial to making this dish, the heat should be low enough so that the egg cooks and sets very gently. Try practising a few times to get the feel of how hot the pan should be; intermittently removing the pan from the heat is a good way to slow the cooking process.

Chicken and prawn spicy garlic don

Don or donburi is a typical Japanese dish of rice, topped with various ingredients. In this version, chicken and prawns are given a fiery kick by the addition of chilli and garlic.

serves 1

75g chicken breast fillet, thinly sliced

cornflour for dusting

olive oil for frying

75g raw peeled tiger prawns

4 small broccoli florets

4 oyster mushrooms

3 asparagus spears, cut into 3cm lengths

1/2 teaspoon chilli garlic sauce (see page 250)

2 tablespoons sake

2 tablespoons Sake soy (see page 248)

a little kuzu or cornflour mixed with water to thicken

freshly ground black pepper

1 teaspoon toasted sesame oil

cooked rice to serve

1   Dust the chicken breast lightly with cornflour and sauté quickly in a little olive oil over high heat in a non-stick frying pan for 1–2 minutes until cooked through. Remove from the pan and keep warm.

2   Repeat the process for the prawns, broccoli, oyster mushrooms and asparagus one at a time, using the same pan and add to the chicken as they are cooked.

3   Again using the same pan, quickly sauté the chilli garlic sauce for a few seconds and then deglaze the pan with sake. Add the Sake soy and, just as it comes to the boil, thicken with the kuzu mixture, and quickly toss the chicken and vegetables into the sauce. Season with the black pepper and add the sesame oil at the last minute.

4   Place the cooked rice in a bowl, spoon the mixture on top and serve.

notes   When making this dish, ensure that you have all the ingredients ready at the start, as it is basically a stir-fry and needs to be done quickly over a high heat.

Try different combinations of meat and fish, or just vegetables, as the sauce goes well with anything.

New-man pasta

Hot noodles in broth are always a favourite, but in this dish we have substituted Italian pasta for noodles to give it a Western twist.

serves 2

vegetable oil for deep-frying
2 garlic cloves, thinly sliced
100g tagliolini or other flat long pasta noodles
sea salt and freshly ground black pepper
2 boneless red snapper fillets, each about 100g
olive oil for frying
100g mixed mushrooms (e.g. shiitake, oyster, cep, chanterelle)
8 green olives
chopped chives for garnish

for the fish broth
440ml Dashi (see page 17) or clear fish stock
3 tablespoons light soy sauce
1/2 teaspoon salt
2 tablespoons sake

1 Make the fish broth by mixing all the ingredients together in a pan and heat gently (do not allow to boil).

2 Bring about 2cm of oil in a saucepan to a temperature of 150°C and slowly deep-fry the garlic slices until they turn a light golden brown. Remove immediately and drain on kitchen paper.

3 Cook the pasta in salted boiling water until just al dente and drain.

4 Preheat a salamander or grill. Brush the snapper fillets with olive oil and season with salt and pepper. Cook under the salamander or grill for 4–5 minutes, until just cooked.

5 At the same time, season the mushrooms with salt and pepper, and sauté in olive oil in a frying pan over medium heat.

6 To serve, quickly reheat the pasta in boiling water for a few seconds, drain and divide between 2 large noodle bowls. Add the mushrooms and olives, and place the snapper fillets on the top. Pour the hot fish broth over the top and sprinkle with chives and the fried garlic.

note Try to get all the ingredients ready at the same time; if not, grill the fish last, so it doesn't overcook.

Tuna with angel hair pasta

Here raw tuna is cut into thin strips, seasoned with sesame, chilli and garlic, and mixed with cold cooked angel hair pasta to make a really interesting combination.

serves 4

90g angel hair pasta (capelli d'angelo)
salt
150g boneless skinless fresh raw tuna
2 tablespoons toasted sesame oil
2 tablespoons olive oil
1 teaspoon chilli garlic sauce (see page 250)
2 tablespoons soy sauce
1/2 bunch of chives, finely chopped

1   Cook the angel hair pasta in plenty of salted boiling water until just al dente. Drain and refresh in cold water, then drain well again.

2   Following the grain of the tuna, slice it into long strips as thin as you can manage (2–3mm).

3   Combine with the drained pasta in a mixing bowl. Add the sesame and olive oils and gently mix again. Add the chilli garlic sauce to the soy sauce and gently mix into the salad, taste and add a little more salt if required.

4   Place on a serving dish and sprinkle with the chives.

desserts

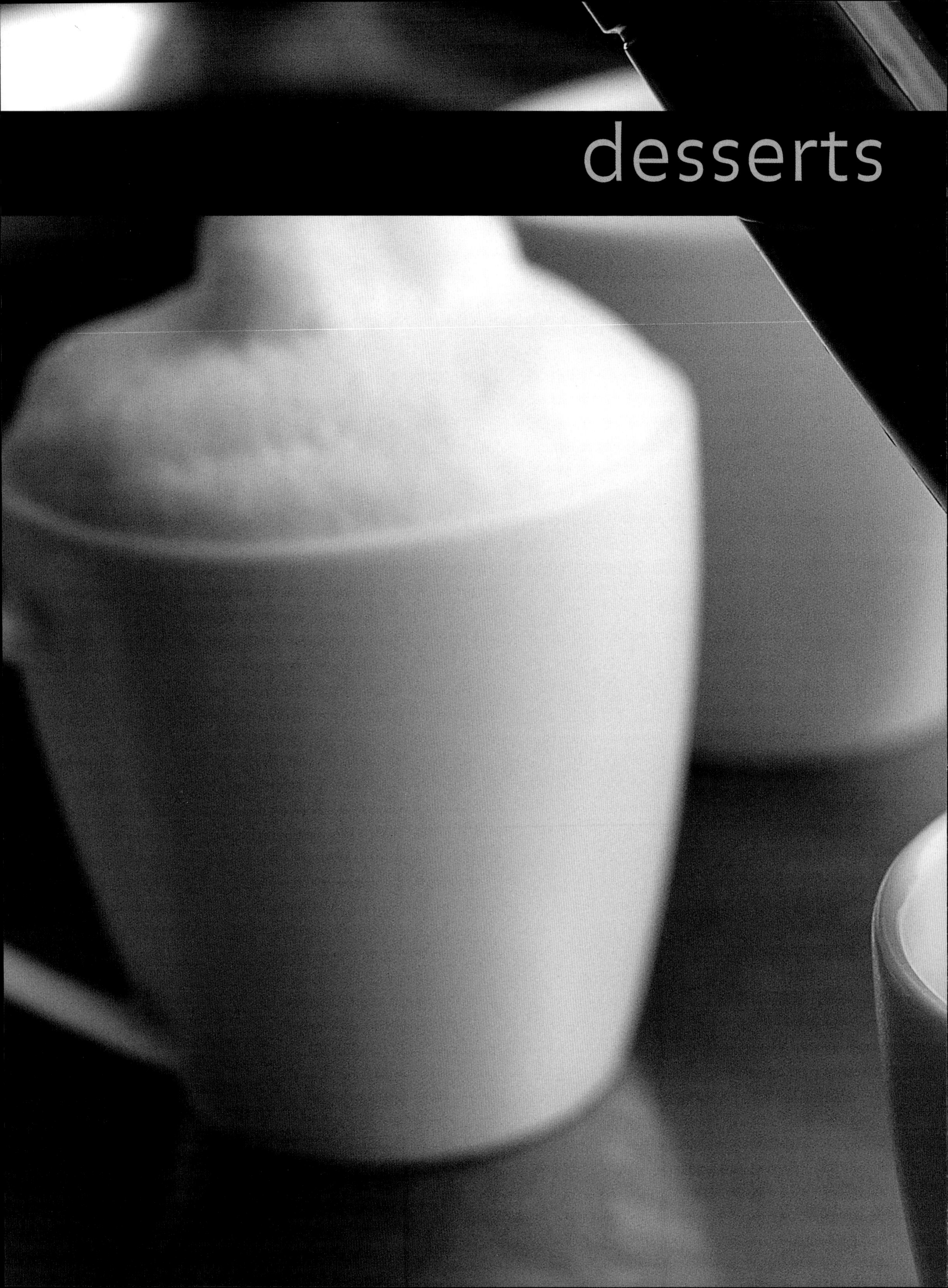

Ice cream tempura

Hot and cold, and soft and crispy, these are the exciting textures and contrasts this dessert presents. The measurements for this are only a rough guide, as it is more of a technique.

serves 2

4 scoops of ice cream in any of your favourite flavours
2 tablespoons cake crumbs
clean unused vegetable oil for deep-frying
flour for dusting
small quantity of Tempura batter (see page 99)
icing sugar for dusting
bamboo leaf to serve (optional)

1 Firstly, scoop the ice cream into balls and then roll these in cake crumbs until the outside is completely coated. Place back in the freezer for 2–3 hours to harden completely.

2 Heat a medium-to-large pan of clean oil (8–10cm deep) to a temperature of 180°C. Remove the ice cream balls from the freezer and quickly roll in the flour and then dip in the tempura batter, making sure that the ice cream is completely covered. Place the battered ice cream balls gently into the oil (only cook 2–3 at a time, so the oil remains hot) and cook for 1 minute per batch, just until the batter is light and crisp. Remove and drain on kitchen paper.

3 Quickly place on a suitable dish, dust with icing sugar and serve immediately, on a bamboo leaf if you like.

note The secret to this dish is to have everything to hand when you are about to fry the ice cream. Two people can make quicker work of the frying, as the ice cream melts quickly, so it needs to be served as soon as possible after cooking.

Mochi ice cream

The wonderful contrast in texture between the soft and chewy sweet mochi balls and their ice cream filling makes this dessert a very special experience. Unusually, in this recipe we measure the water by weight for precision.

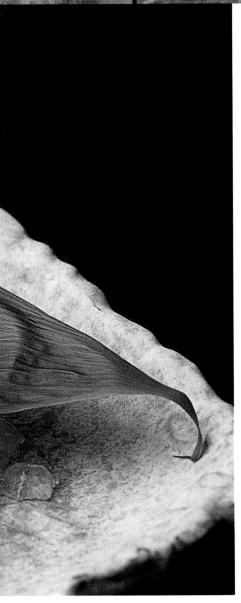

makes 15–20

95g caster sugar
210g water
100g mochi flour (Japanese rice flour, see page 252)
cornflour for dusting
400g good-quality ice cream, any flavour(s), softened in the
  refrigerator for 20 minutes

to serve
bamboo leaves, crushed ice and fresh seasonal berries

1 In a microwavable bowl, dissolve the sugar in the water and mix in the mochi flour, ensuring there are no lumps. Cook in the microwave oven on medium heat for 30 seconds. Remove and beat vigorously with a wooden spoon (the mix will become stiff and elastic). Place back in the microwave oven and repeat the process three more times. Turn out on a board dusted with cornflour and let cool.

2 Scoop the ice cream into small balls using a melon baller (maximum diameter 2cm) and place back in the freezer.

3 When the paste is cool, roll it out into a sheet about 3mm thick, dusting it with cornflour to prevent sticking. Place on a tray and freeze for about 30 minutes to harden.

4 Remove the mochi paste sheet from the freezer and, using a 4–5cm diameter cutter, cut out as many rounds as you can. Place an ice cream ball in the centre of each and wrap it in the mochi paste, then place back in the freezer.

5 About 3–5 minutes before serving, remove from the freezer to allow the mochi to soften slightly.

6 Serve on bamboo leaves set on top of a plate of crushed ice and decorate with fresh seasonal berries.

note Make green tea- or chocolate-flavoured mochi by replacing 10g of mochi flour with green tea powder or cocoa powder.

Chocolate satandagi

This consists of a very light hot chocolate doughnut with a soft chocolate centre, served with Almond ice cream. It might be an idea to warn your guests to be careful when eating the satandagi, as the chocolate inside the doughnut is very liquid.

serves 4–6

vegetable oil for deep-frying
shelled pistachio nuts to serve
raspberry purée to decorate (optional)

for the Almond ice cream
200ml double cream
200ml milk
5 egg yolks
75g caster sugar
150g finely ground almonds

for the Chocolate ganache
150g dark chocolate (about 66% cocoa solids)
150ml double cream

for the batter
2 egg yolks
50g caster sugar
130ml milk
160g flour
whites of 3 eggs

1   To make the ice cream, heat the cream and milk to just below boiling point. Whisk the egg yolks and sugar to together in a large bowl. Pour the hot milk and cream mixture on the egg yolks and sugar, whisking continuously, then return to a clean saucepan. Cook over a gentle heat, stirring continuously, until the mixture begins to thicken slightly (do not allow to boil or the egg yolks will be scrambled in the custard). Remove from the heat, whisk in the ground almonds and allow to cool completely. Strain the mixture into an ice cream machine and freeze according to the manufacturer's instructions.

2   To make the ganache, break the chocolate into small chunks and place in a heatproof bowl. Heat the cream in a saucepan to just below boiling point and remove from the heat. Pour the cream on the chocolate and stir gently to mix in as the chocolate melts. Allow the ganache to cool and refrigerate. When cold, scoop into tablespoon-sized pieces and place in the freezer to freeze solid.

3   To make the batter, whisk 2 egg yolks with 20g caster sugar in a large bowl. Whisk in the milk, followed by the flour, a little at a time, ensuring there are no lumps. In another large bowl, whisk the egg whites and the remaining caster sugar to form a meringue, then fold this gently into the batter mixture.

4   Heat a medium-to-large pan of oil (8–10cm deep) to a temperature of 160°C. Place a bamboo skewer into each of the frozen ganache scoops, then use the skewer to dip the ganache into the batter, making sure that it is completely covered. Dip into the hot oil and cook for 2 minutes, then remove and drain on kitchen paper.

5   Transfer to a suitable serving dish and serve with the Almond ice cream and sprinkled with pistachio nuts. If you like, you can give the plate a dash of colour with a few splashes of raspberry purée.

note   You can make the Chocolate ganache well in advance and store in the freezer.

Chestnut brûlée with chocolate sorbet and tonka bean foam

Here a brûlée of chestnut-flavoured cream is complemented by a rich dark chocolate sorbet and finished with an aromatic tonka bean foam.

serves 6

for the Tonka bean foam
35g egg yolk
30g egg whites
60g caster sugar
125g milk
125g whipping cream
15g tonka beans (see page 253)
5g nibbed cocoa
1/2 vanilla pod
1/2 leaf gelatine

for the Chocolate sorbet
200g dark chocolate (minimum 70% cocoa solids)
250ml water
130g sugar
50g liquid glucose

for the Chestnut brûlée
30g egg yolks
30g caster sugar
100g double cream
220g chestnut purée

to decorate
Dried apple slices (see page 232)
marrons glacés

1   To make the Tonka bean foam, whisk the egg yolks and whites and the sugar together in a bowl. Place the milk, cream, tonka beans and cocoa nibs in a saucepan. Split the vanilla pod and scrape out the seeds, add these and the pod to the milk, and slowly heat until just boiling.

2   Pour the milk and cream mixture on to the egg and sugar, and whisk together. Return to the saucepan and cook over a low heat until the mix thickens slightly, or to a maximum of 180°C and remove from the heat.

3   Soak the gelatine in a little water, then add to the lukewarm mixture and allow to cool. When completely cold, whisk to a smooth liquid and place in a cream gun. Fill with gas according to the manufacturer's instructions and refrigerate.

4   To make the Chocolate sorbet, break the chocolate into small pieces and place in a large bowl. Warm the water, sugar and glucose together in a saucepan until they dissolve and then heat to 180°C. Pour on to the chocolate and stir gently until the chocolate has melted and completely blended. Allow the mixture to cool, then churn in an ice cream machine according to the manufacturer's instructions and place in the freezer.

5   To make the Chestnut brûlée, preheat the oven to 190°C/gas 5. Whisk together the egg yolks and sugar. Heat the cream in a saucepan to just below boiling point and pour on to the eggs and sugar, whisking together. Blend the chestnut purée into the cream and egg mixture until completely smooth. Pour the mixture into suitable heatproof serving dishes, place in a hot-water bath and cook in the oven for 40 minutes. Remove and allow to cool, then refrigerate until ready to serve.

6   To serve, place a scoop of sorbet on the top of the brûlée, partly cover with the Tonka bean foam and garnish with some Dried apple slices and marrons glacés.

note   If tonka beans are not available, try replacing them with vanilla and almond essence, plus a pinch of cinnamon.

Apricot and jasmine soup with peanut crunch and beer ice cream

This dessert has an unusual combination of a salted peanut crunch with an apricot sauce infused with jasmine. When eaten with the malty flavour of beer ice cream it produces a wonderful range of flavour sensations.

serves 6–8

for the Apricot and jasmine soup
2 tablespoons sugar
2 tablespoons water
5g jasmine tea
250g apricot purée

for the Beer ice cream
100ml double cream
150ml milk
6 egg yolks
150g caster sugar
250ml beer (any malt or lager-type beer)

for the Peanut crunch
90g butter
40g caster sugar
60g light brown sugar
100g peanut butter
50g unsalted roasted peanuts
50g unsalted roasted hazelnuts
1 teaspoon Maldon sea salt
1 teaspoon baking powder
150g bread flour

to decorate
Dried apple slices (see page 232)
shiso leaves

1   You need to make the soup the day before: warm the sugar with the water until the sugar has dissolved, then mix with the jasmine tea. Whisk the apricot purée into the tea mixture and allow to infuse overnight.

2   To make the ice cream, heat the cream and milk to just below boiling point. Whisk the egg yolks and sugar to together in a large bowl. Pour the hot milk and cream mixture on to the egg yolks and sugar, whisking continuously, then return to a clean saucepan. Cook over a gentle heat, stirring continuously, until the mixture begins to thicken slightly (do not allow to boil or the egg yolks will be scrambled in the custard). Remove from the heat and allow to cool.

3   Mix the beer into the mixture, place in an ice cream machine and freeze according to the manufacturer's instructions.

4   To make the peanut crunch, soften the butter and cream together in a mixing bowl with the caster sugar, brown sugar and peanut butter. Gently mix in the rest of the ingredients, roll up the mix in clingfilm and chill until set.

5   Preheat the oven to 180°C/gas 4 and cut the (now solid) peanut crunch dough into 1cm thick slices. Place on a non-stick baking sheet and cook for 8–12 minutes in the oven. Allow to cool and break into rough chunks.

6   To serve, place a little of the peanut crunch into each serving bowl and top with a scoop of the ice cream. Strain a little of the soup into the bottom of the bowl and finish with a dried apple slice and a shiso leaf.

Nashi pear gyoza with passion fruit sauce

These are essentially pot sticker dumplings with a sweet filling. In Japan, they are normally made with a savoury filling, but they also make an excellent dessert. In this recipe, the filling is Asian pear combined with pecan nuts and fresh mint, and they are served with a passion fruit dipping sauce.

makes 16–20 (serves 3–4)

50g demerara sugar
200g Nashi Asian pears, peeled, cored and diced
finely grated or pared zest of 2 lemons and juice of ¹/₂ lemon
25g shelled pecan nuts
10 fresh mint leaves
16–20 gyoza or wonton wrappers
100ml passion fruit purée
olive oil for cooking
2–4 drops of toasted sesame oil

1   Place the sugar, pears, lemon zest and juice in a small bowl, cover with clingfilm and steam for 20 minutes. Remove the contents and strain off the liquor. Allow to cool and keep aside.

2   Chop the pecan nuts and the mint, and stir these into the pear mix.

3   To make the gyoza, lay a gyoza or wonton wrapper in front of you, moisten the edge of the dough with a little water, put a spoonful of pear mix in the centre of each wrapper and fold it over the top of the mix to make a semicircle. Seal the edge by making little folds and squeeze the ends together. Repeat the process until all the mix has been used up.

4   Make the dipping sauce by mixing the juice left from the steaming of the pear with the passion fruit purée and a little water if too thick.

5   Place a small amount of olive oil in a non-stick saucepan over a medium heat and cook the gyozas, flat end down, in the pan. When the bottom just begins to brown, add 3 tablespoons of water and 2 drops of sesame oil to the pan, turn the heat to full and cover with a lid to let the gyoza steam for 2–3 minutes, until all the water has evaporated. Repeat the process for any remaining gyoza.

6   Serve the gyoza on a suitable dish while still hot, with the browned side upright and a dipping bowl of the passion fruit purée.

note   You can make different fillings for the dumplings using any hard fruits, such as pineapple, ordinary pear or apple.

Summer fruit sake jelly

This dish is on the menus of our London restaurants when there is an abundance of berry fruit, and it makes a light and delightful end to a meal. It may be made with any of your favourite summer fruits – strawberries, wild strawberries, raspberries, blackcurrants, redcurrants or rowan berries.

makes 24 spoonful servings

100g selection of summer berries
2 gelatine leaves
50g caster sugar
100ml sake
fresh mint to garnish

1   Wash the fruit gently, drain well and place on kitchen paper to absorb excess moisture.

2   Place the gelatine leaves in a non-reactive bowl and add 100ml water and the sugar. Warm the bowl gently, preferably over a saucepan of hot water, and stir slowly until all the sugar and gelatine have dissolved. Set aside to cool slightly.

3   When the mixture is tepid, stir in the sake and strain the mixture through a fine sieve to remove any remaining small lumps of gelatine.

4   Pour a little of the mixture into the base of the mould (see note opposite) or spoon to cover the bottom, and place in the freezer for a few minutes to set.

5   Remove the mould from the freezer, place the fruit on top of the set jelly and cover with the remaining jelly mixture. Place in the refrigerator and allow to set for 3–4 hours.

6   When the jelly is fully set, if using a mould, run a little warm water over the base of the mould and turn out the jelly out on your serving dish. Garnish with mint sprigs.

note   When we make these jellies in the restaurant, we use a rubber mould designed for making mini chocolates. If you don't have access to something like this you can use one big mould, as this makes it easier to turn the jelly out. If you are using little moulds, when unmoulding first place the jellies in the freezer to set a little harder, as this will help make them easier to turn out. Don't worry if they freeze, as when you have turned them out the jelly will become clear again as they defrost.

Plum wine tagliatelle

Japanese *Umeshu* or plum wine is made from a species of plum that actually has more resemblance to an apricot. It has a sweet, smooth flavour and, in this recipe, is set into a jelly almost like a cold sweet noodle.

serves 4

1 gelatine leaf
400ml Japanese plum wine
8g agar agar
shiso sprigs to decorate

1   Soak the gelatine leaf in a little cold water for 2 minutes.

2   Mix the plum wine and agar agar in a small pan and bring just the boil, then whisk in the gelatine leaf until dissolved. Pour the mixture into a flat stainless-steel tray to a depth of about 3mm and put in the refrigerator to set for 3–4 hours. (Make sure the tray is level so that the liquid sets to an even thickness.)

3   When ready to serve, remove the tray from the refrigerator and make cuts lengthways with a pizza wheel or knife to produce strips of jelly that resemble tagliatelle. Wipe the underside of the tray with a cloth dipped in hot water to help loosen the tagliatelle and place in suitable bowls. Garnish with shiso sprigs.

notes   In summer, serve these as quickly as possible as the noodles will melt.

You may sprinkle a little fruit juice or more plum wine on the tagliatelle when serving, if you like.

Agar agar, or *kanten* in Japan, is produced from seaweed and has a neutral smell and taste. It can be bought in powder form.

Whisky cappuccino

This dessert is layered with a wonderful array of textures and flavours, from an intense coffee brûlée and a cocoa crunch through to iced milk and cream, and then the luxurious topping of whisky foam.

makes 8 cups

for the Iced milk and cream
50g sugar
1 tablespoon milk powder
50g double cream
175g milk

for the Cocoa crunch
50g sugar
50g butter
50g ground almonds
5g cocoa powder
40g flour
10g crushed coffee beans

for the whisky foam
150g milk
25g double cream
20g sugar
2/3 gelatine leaf
3 tablespoons whisky

for the Coffee brûlée
60g egg yolk
50g sugar
50g milk
20g coffee paste or triple strength espresso coffee
200ml whipping cream

1   First make the Iced milk and cream by mixing together the sugar, milk powder, cream and milk in a saucepan. Bring to the boil over a medium heat, allow to cool slightly and liquidize for a few seconds. Strain and refrigerate. When cold, churn in an ice cream machine according to the manufacturer's instructions.

2   For the Cocoa crunch, beat together the sugar and butter until light and creamy. Fold in the almonds, followed by the rest of the ingredients, until completely incorporated. Then place the mixture in the freezer for 15 minutes until solid.

3   Preheat the oven to 180°C/gas 4. Grate the frozen Cocoa crunch mixture on to a non-stick baking sheet no more than 3mm in height and cook in the oven for 7–10 minutes. Allow to cool and then break into rough chunks.

4   For the Whisky foam topping, bring to the boil quickly the milk, cream and sugar, then remove from the heat. Soak the gelatine in a little cold water, whisk it into the milk and cream mixture along with the whisky, while it is still lukewarm, then allow to set. When completely cold, whisk it into a smooth liquid and place in a cream gun. Fill with gas according to the manufacturer's instructions.

5   For the Coffee brûlée, preheat the oven to 110°C/gas 1/4, then whisk together the egg yolk and sugar in a heatproof bowl. In a saucepan, bring the milk, coffee and whipping cream just to the boil and then whisk on to the egg yolk and sugar. Strain the mixture into 8 cappuccino cups, filling them only one-third of the way up, and place in a baking tray filled with hot water. Place in the oven for 25 minutes. When set, allow to cool and then refrigerate.

6   To serve, place a little of the Cocoa crunch into each of the cups on top of the brûlée, followed by a scoop of the Iced milk and cream. Then top with the Whisky foam to resemble a cappuccino. Eat with teaspoons.

cocktails

Lychee martini

This cocktail is best when it is served with a fresh lychee in it, and even better if served with the Thai Dragon lychee, when it is in season. If you can't find fresh lychees, any canned type can be substituted.

makes 1

25ml lychee liqueur
25ml vanilla vodka
25 ml mandarin vodka
15ml passion fruit juice
splash of fresh lime juice
ice cubes
fresh or canned lychee for garnish (see above)

1   Pour the liquids into a cocktail shaker full of ice cubes and shake well for 20 seconds.

2   Pour into a chilled martini glass, garnish with a lychee and serve.

Pineapple martini

This refreshing summer martini is full of tropical pineapple flavour and has proved incredibly popular, especially with the ladies, in our London restaurants.

serves 1

30ml pineapple vodka
30ml peach schnapps
20ml pineapple purée
dash of lemon juice
dash of sirop de gomme (sugar syrup)
ice cubes

1   Pour the liquids into a cocktail shaker full of ice cubes and shake well for 20 seconds.

2   Pour into a chilled martini or other suitable glass.

Apple martini

This very popular version of the martini has a slightly sour twist to it that brings out the apple flavours. The dried apple slices are an optional extra, but they are also great on fruit salads or with ice cream.

makes 1

40ml sour apple schnapps
35ml vodka
20ml apple juice
good splash of fresh lime juice
ice cubes

for the Dried apple slice (optional)
1 Granny Smith apple, cored but unpeeled
squeeze of lemon juice

1   If using the dried apple slices, you need to make them well ahead. Slice the apple across very thinly on a mandolin grater (the slices should be no more than 1mm thick) and place the slices in a bowl of water with a squeeze of lemon juice. Remove from the water and pat dry, then place on a non-stick baking sheet. Place the baking sheet into a very cool oven (110°C/gas1/4) and leave for around 6 hours, checking and turning at hourly intervals to ensure that the slices dry uniformly but do not colour.

2   To make the martini, pour the liquids into a cocktail shaker full of ice cubes, shake well for 20 seconds and pour into a chilled martini glass. Garnish with a dried apple slice, if you like, and serve immediately.

Watermelon martini

This very refreshing version of the martini uses fresh watermelon juice. Shochu is a Japanese clear spirit rather like vodka.

serves 1

25ml vodka
10ml shochu (see above)
25ml melon schnapps
30ml fresh watermelon juice (see note)
dash of sirop de gomme (sugar syrup)
dash of fresh lime juice
ice cubes
wedge of watermelon for garnish

1   Place all the ingredients into a cocktail shaker and shake for 20 seconds.

2   Strain into a martini glass and garnish with a slice of watermelon.

note   The best way to make the watermelon juice is to chop up some watermelon flesh and place it in a cocktail shaker and press it with the end of a rolling pin to squeeze out the juice.

Tokyo peach cocktail

This is a simple and refreshing take on the classic Bellini.

serves 1

10ml Crème de Peche
20ml Calpico (see note)
10ml peach purée
chilled Champagne to top up

1   Place all the ingredients except the champagne in a cocktail shaker with some ice cubes and shake for 20 seconds.

2   Strain into a champagne glass and top up with Champagne.

note   Calpico is a concentrated cultured milk drink with a slightly citrusy flavour that is very popular in Japan. Japanese food stores will have it in tins.

Midori margarita

The addition of Midori, a Japanese melon liqueur makes this Margarita rather special. It does not, however, suit the normal garnish of salt.

serves 1

ice cubes
25ml Triple Sec
25ml Midori
25ml tequila
dash of fresh lime juice
lime wedge for garnish

1   Place some ice cubes and all the liquids into a cocktail shaker and shake for 20 seconds.

2   Strain into a glass filled with ice cubes and garnish with a lime wedge.

Japanese mojito

Our twist on the classic Cuban mojito uses vodka instead of rum, and fresh shiso leaves along with mint, together with a hint of vanilla, which creates an interesting flavour combination.

serves 1

20ml sirop de gomme (sugar syrup)
1 drop of vanilla essence
6 fresh shiso leaves
8 fresh mint leaves, plus more for garnish
15ml fresh lime juice
crushed ice
50ml vodka

1   Place the syrup, vanilla and 4 shiso leaves in a liquidizer and blend together.

2   Muddle the remaining shiso leaves, mint leaves and lime juice in a tall glass and fill with crushed ice.

3   Pour in the syrup mixture and the vodka, and stir.

Sake mule

This twist on the classic '40s cocktail, using sake instead of vodka, has a spicy kick to it.

serves 1

1 slice of fresh root ginger
1/2 lemon grass stalk, plus another crushed stalk for garnish
2 shiso leaves
50ml sake
splash of kalamansi juice (see page 251) or lime juice
10ml sirop de gomme (sugar syrup)
10ml elderflower cordial
dash of runny honey
crushed ice
splash of ginger beer

1   In a cocktail shaker, muddle the root ginger, lemon grass and shiso leaves.

2   Add the rest of the ingredients apart from the ginger beer, and shake.

3   Strain into a glass filled with more crushed ice, top up with the ginger beer and garnish with the crushed lemon grass stalk.

note   The kalamansi, or sour lime, looks like a green tangerine but has a very sour taste.

Japanese bloody Mary

Our version of the Bloody Mary is made using wasabi instead of horseradish, to give it a subtly different kick.

serves 1

50ml vodka
10ml yuzu or lemon juice
dash of Japanese tonkatsu sauce (see page 253) or
  Worcestershire sauce
1/2 teaspoon wasabi paste
freshly ground black pepper
tomato juice to top up
ice cubes
cucumber wedge for garnish
shiso leaf for garnish

1   Mix together the vodka, yuzu or lemon juice, tonkatsu or Worcestershire sauce, wasabi and black pepper to taste, then top up with tomato juice to taste.

2   Pour over ice cubes in a cocktail glass and garnish with the cucumber wedge and shiso leaf.

Orange Ki

This cocktail is a perfectly matched combination of orange, apple, almond, cinnamon and whiskey, shaken with ice.

serves 1

10ml sirop de gomme (sugar syrup)
1/2 teaspoon ground cinnamon
2 orange wedges
25ml Jack Daniel's
25ml Amaretto
30ml fresh apple juice
crushed ice
dash of Kahlúa
1 cinnamon stick for garnish

1   In a cocktail shaker, muddle the syrup, ground cinnamon and orange wedges together.

2   Pour in the Jack Daniel's, Amaretto and apple juice, and shake with crushed ice.

3   Strain into a glass filled with more crushed ice, pour a little Kahlúa on the top and garnish with a cinnamon stick.

sauces

dressings

Jalapeño dressing

10g chopped jalapeño chilli
1 teaspoon sea salt
1 teaspoon chopped garlic
100ml rice vinegar
120ml grapeseed oil

1   In a food processor, process the jalapeño, salt, garlic and vinegar until well mixed and the chilli is finely chopped.

2   Slowly add the grapeseed oil and process until well blended.

Spicy lemon dressing

100ml freshly squeezed lemon juice
3 tablespoons plus 1 teaspoon soy sauce
1 heaped teaspoon finely chopped garlic
1/2 teaspoon chilli garlic sauce (page 250)
1 teaspoon sea salt
1/2 teaspoon freshly ground black pepper
140ml grapeseed oil

1   In a bowl, mix together all the ingredients except the oil. Mix well to dissolve the salt.

2   Mix in the oil.

Matsuhisa dressing

140g finely chopped onion
4 tablespoons plus 2 teaspoons soy sauce
2 tablespoons plus 1 teaspoon rice vinegar
1 teaspoon caster sugar
1/2 teaspoon Japanese mustard powder (or English mustard powder)
sea salt and freshly ground black pepper
4 teaspoons water
2 tablespoons plus 1 teaspoon toasted sesame oil
2 tablespoons plus 1 teaspoon grapeseed oil

1   Rinse the onion in cold water to remove the sharpness, then drain well.

2   In a mixing bowl, mix together the drained onion, soy sauce, vinegar, sugar, mustard powder, salt, pepper and water.

3   When the salt has dissolved, mix in the sesame and grapeseed oils, a little at a time.

note   This dressing develops a better flavour when made the day before.

Spicy lemon and caper dressing

25g salt-packed capers
100ml Spicy lemon dressing (opposite)

1   Rinse the capers well under cold running water to remove the salt, then drain.

2   Finely chop the capers.

3   Mix well with the Spicy lemon dressing.

Watercress dressing

35g watercress leaves and stalks
1 heaped teaspoon salt
$1/2$ teaspoon freshly ground black pepper
4 tablespoons rice vinegar
2 tablespoons grapeseed oil

1   Coarsely chop the watercress.

2   Place this and all the other ingredients in a food processor and blend.

salsas

Ginger salsa

100g finely chopped red onion
25g finely chopped root ginger
100ml Tosa-zu sauce (see page 31)

Combine all the ingredients and mix well.

Jalapeño salsa

10g finely chopped jalapeño chilli
100g finely chopped white onion
1 tablespoon plus 1 teaspoon olive oil
4 tablespoons lemon juice
$2/3$ teaspoon salt

Combine all the ingredients and mix well.

Dashi ponzu

50ml Dashi (page 249)
50ml Ponzu (page 248)

Combine the liquids together and mix well.

Yuzu ponzu dressing

5 tablespoons Ponzu (see page 248)
1 tablespoon yuzu juice (see page 253)

Combine the ingredients together in a bowl and mix well.

Den miso

100ml sake
100ml mirin
300g white miso paste (see page 253)
150g granulated sugar

1   Put the sake and mirin in a non-reactive saucepan and bring to the boil for 2–3 minutes to evaporate off the alcohol.

2   Over a medium heat, add the miso paste to the pan a little at a time, to blend it into a smooth sauce.

3   Turn up the heat and add the sugar in 2 or 3 lots and continue stirring so the mixture does not burn.

4   When the sugar has completely dissolved, remove from the heat and allow to cool to room temperature. This will keep in the fridge for up to 3 months.

Shiso ponzu

1 tablespoon green Tabasco sauce
1 tablespoon soy sauce
1 tablespoon shiso vinegar or rice vinegar
1 tablespoon grapeseed oil
1 tablespoon lime juice
2 teaspoons finely chopped red chilli
1^{1}/2 tablespoons finely chopped white onion
1 tablespoon finely chopped shiso or coriander leaves

Combine all the ingredients together in a bowl and mix well.

note   Only add the chopped shiso or coriander leaf at the last minute, otherwise they will turn brown if added more than 20 minutes ahead of use.

Spicy miso

100ml sake
100ml mirin
150g red miso paste (see page 252)
150g white miso paste (see page 253)
150g granulated sugar
1/2 teaspoon shichimi togarashi (see page 252)
2 tablespoons chilli oil
1 tablespoon toasted sesame oil
100ml water

1 Put the sake and mirin in a non-reactive saucepan and bring to the boil to evaporate off the alcohol.

2 Lower the heat to medium and add the miso pastes, a little at a time, to blend to a smooth sauce.

3 Turn up the heat and add the sugar in 2 or 3 lots, continuing to stir so the mixture does not burn. When the sugar has completely dissolved, remove from the heat and allow to cool to room temperature.

4 When cool, whisk in the shichimi, chilli oil, sesame oil and water just before using. This will keep in the fridge for up to 3 months.

Jalapeño ponzu

100ml Jalapeño dressing (page 242)
100ml Ponzu (page 248)

Mix the two ingredients well together in a bowl.

New-style oil

3 tablespoons light olive oil
1 teaspoon toasted sesame oil

Combine the two ingredients together.

note This can be made ahead of time and will keep for up to a week, but once it has been heated it should be discarded as heating burns the sesame oil.

Red anticucho sauce

1/2 teaspoon dried oregano
*2 tablespoons plus 1 teaspoon Aji Panca (Peruvian
   red chilli paste, see page 250)*
3 tablespoons plus 1 teaspoon rice vinegar
1 teaspoon finely chopped garlic
1 teaspoon ground cumin
2 tablespoons sake
1 teaspoon sea salt
1 teaspoon freshly ground black pepper
2 tablespoons grapeseed oil

1   Crush the oregano using a pestle and
mortar to release its aroma.

2   Combine this with all the other
ingredients except the oil and mix well to
dissolve the salt.

3   Then mix in the oil.

Spicy black bean sauce

1 tablespoon black bean paste
5 tablespoons sake
1 tablespoon light soy sauce
1/2 teaspoon chilli garlic sauce (see page 250)

Mix all the ingredients together well in a
bowl.

Spicy sour sauce

100ml fresh lemon juice
3 teaspoons soy sauce
2 teaspoons mirin
1 teaspoon chilli garlic sauce (see page 250)

Combine all the ingredients and mix well
together.

Creamy spicy sauce

1 fresh egg yolk
1 teaspoon sea salt
pinch of freshly ground white pepper
1 teaspoon rice vinegar
6 tablespoons grapeseed or vegetable oil
1 teaspoon chilli garlic sauce (see page 250)

1   Put the egg yolk in a small bowl. Add the
salt, white pepper and rice vinegar, and mix
well.

2   Add the oil gradually, drop by drop at
first but faster as you proceed, and whisk
constantly.

3   Add the chilli garlic sauce and mix well.

note   You can use ready-made mayonnaise
instead of making your own and simply mix
that with chilli garlic sauce; if using fresh egg,
only make it when it is needed and use it
immediately.

Ceviche sauce

2 teaspoons Aji Amarillo (yellow or orange chilli paste, see page 250)
120ml fresh lemon juice
4 teaspoons yuzu juice (see page 253)
2 teaspoons soy sauce
1 teaspoon black pepper
2 teaspoons finely chopped garlic
1 teaspoon finely chopped root ginger
4 teaspoons salted water

Put all ingredients into a bowl and mix well until smooth and blended.

Balsamic teriyaki sauce

250ml balsamic vinegar
300ml chicken stock
50g granulated sugar
3 tablespoons and 1 teaspoon soy sauce
3 tablespoons and 1 teaspoon mirin
kuzu, arrowroot or cornflour mixed with a little water to thicken

1   Put the balsamic vinegar into a non-reactive saucepan and boil until it has reduced by two-thirds.

2   Add the stock, sugar, soy sauce and mirin, and heat gently until the sugar dissolves. Bring quickly to the boil and whisk in the kuzu to thicken.

3   Use while still hot. Any not used will keep in the fridge for up to 3 days.

note   It is not necessary to use an expensive balsamic vinegar as the flavour is intensified during the reduction.

Mustard miso

1 teaspoon Japanese mustard powder (or English mustard powder)
2 teaspoons hot water
150g Den miso (see page 244)
2 tablespoons plus 1 teaspoon rice vinegar

1   In a small bowl, mix the mustard powder with the hot water into a smooth paste, then cover with clingfilm and leave for an hour to allow the mustard to develop its piquancy.

2   Mix in the rest of the ingredients to form a smooth sauce.

Spicy lemon and garlic sauce

200ml sake
2 tablespoons plus 2 teaspoons soy sauce
1 teaspoon chilli garlic sauce (see page 250)
1 large teaspoon finely chopped garlic
1/2 teaspoon finely chopped root ginger
2 tablespoons plus 1 teaspoon fresh lemon juice
1 tablespoon yuzu juice (see page 253)
2 tablespoons grapeseed oil
2 tablespoons olive oil

1   Heat the sake in a saucepan to allow some of the alcohol to evaporate off. Let cool to room temperature.

2   Mix this and all the other ingredients well together in a bowl. This will keep in the fridge for up to a week.

Yuzu soy

5 tablespoons soy sauce
2 tablespoons yuzu juice (see page 253)

Combine the liquids together in a bowl and mix well. Store in the refrigerator for up to a week.

Sake soy

150ml sake
5 tablespoons soy sauce

Combine the liquids together and mix well.

Ponzu

4 tablespoons soy sauce
8 tablespoons rice vinegar
4 tablespoons lemon juice
about 2cm square piece of konbu (see page 251)

1   Mix the ingredients together in a bowl and leave overnight to infuse.

2   Next day, remove the konbu before use.

Ama zu ponzu

3 tablespoons rice vinegar
5 tablespoons Ponzu (opposite)
2 tablespoons caster sugar
1¹/₂ teaspoons salt

In a saucepan over a low heat, gently heat the rice vinegar, Ponzu, sugar and salt until the sugar has dissolved, then remove from the heat and allow to cool.

Dried miso

100g red miso (aka miso)

1   With a palette knife, spread the miso as thinly as possible on a silicone or non-stick baking sheet and place in a warm area to dry out naturally (24–48 hours).

2   Scrape the miso into a bowl and crush to a powder.

notes   The process can be speeded up by placing the sheet in a cool oven (110°C/gas ¹/₄) for 1–2 hours, but care must be taken that the miso does not become too dark.
   Drying times may vary according to the time of the year.

Dashi

1 litre water
10g konbu (see page 251)
30g dried bonito flakes (see page 250)

1   Heat the water and konbu together slowly in a saucepan over a medium heat.

2   Just before the water boils, take out the konbu, add the bonito flakes and turn off the heat.

3   Leave the stock until the bonito flakes have sunk to the bottom of the pan and then strain.

Glossary

aji amarillo
This dried chilli is orange, wrinkled, and tapers to a point. Its fruity flavour makes it suitable for chilli sauces and stews. Aji amarillo paste is available as a commercial product in shops selling ingredients for South American cooking.

aji panca
This dried chilli is dark brown, wrinkled and tapers to a point. Its berry flavour and fruit tones make it suitable for chilli sauces and fish dishes. Aji panca paste is available as a commercial product in shops selling ingredients for South American cooking.

aonori laver
Green seaweed, see Nori.

asari clams
Also known as the Manila or short-necked clam, these small clams are very popular in Japan for their tenderness and sweetness.

asatsuki chives
Similar to Chinese chives and spring onions, asatsuki chives (*Allium ledebourianum*) can be shallow-fried as a vegetable or used as seasoning with sashimi.

ayu
This river fish (*Plecoglossus altivelis*) is caught with rod and line from June through August. Large specimens can be as long as 30cm, but most are not even half that size. Ayu is usually eaten grilled or broiled with salt.

ayu tade
A peppery herb often used in the cooking of the ayu river fish. See Tade.

bamboo shoot skin
Known as *take-no-ko* in Japanese, the shoots of both the *Phyllostachys heterocycla* and *P. bambusoides* are a popular delicacy in Japan. The skin, which is usually peeled away before the shoots are boiled, can be used as an attractive garnish with strong hints of late spring, as are the plant's leaves.

bayberries
The purplish red fruit of the bayberry tree (*Myrica rubra*) is in season from late June to early July. The berries can be eaten raw, pickled in salt or made into jam or a liqueur.

black cod
Also known as sablefish, black cod (*Anoplopoma fimbria*) is a dark-coloured marine fish which is caught in North American Pacific waters from the Bering Sea to Isla Cedros, Baja California. Black cod can reach a length of 90cm and average 9kg in weight. Due to its rich oil content, it is exceptionally flavourful and an excellent fish for smoking. Despite its name, this fish is not in fact actually a member of the cod family.

black rice
Black rice is a glutinous and ancient variety of Japanese rice with a purple-black pigment in the rice bran. It has a concentrated flavour.

bonito flakes
Filleted bonito is steamed, dried, smoked and cured with a mould (*Aspergillus glaucus*). When the fillets have become as hard as a piece of wood, they are shaved. This whole process takes many months. The flakes are used to make dashi and as a flavouring and garnish in numerous other dishes. In fact, dried bonito flakes are necessary in one way or another for making every Japanese meal. They are called *katsuobushi* in Japanese.

buckwheat
Called soba in Japanese, this herbaceous plant (*Fagopyrum esculentum*) is cultivated for its groats. The husk is removed and used as a filling for pillows. The groats are ground into the flour that is used to make soba noodles. Groats can also be cooked with rice or used for making beer or vodka.

chilli garlic sauce
This fiery sauce is made from a blend of fresh, roasted or dried chillies and garlic, sugar, salt, vinegar and other seasonings. It is called *tobanjan* in Japanese.

daikon
The giant white radish (*Raphanus sativus*) is an essential ingredient in the Japanese larder. Grated daikon is added to the tempura dipping sauce because it aids the digestion of oily foods. Daikons are often cut lengthways into a continuous sheet, using a special grater called a *katsuramuki*, for use in various preparations.
The young shoots of the daikon, or daikon cress, are used in salads and as a garnish for sushi. See Kaiware.

dashi
Japanese stock is made from dried bonito flakes and konbu. With soy sauce, saké and miso, it is one of the most important elements in Japanese cooking. (See pages 17 and 249.)

edamame
The Japanese term for fresh green soy beans.

enoki mushrooms
This winter mushroom (*Flammulina velutipes*) grows naturally worldwide, yet is known almost exclusively by its Japanese name. The sticky yellow-white cap is seldom wider than 1cm, while the long, thin stalks are usually well over 12cm. Enoki mushrooms are used in soups, stews, and grilled with chicken. Fresh enoki are exported from Japan in sealed plastic packets that keep them fresh for a time.

eringi mushrooms
(pleurote du panicaut)
Pleurotus eryngii is a wild mushroom with a dark brown cap to be found between June and October, growing to a height of between 7 and 20cm. Its flesh is firm and fragrant.

flying fish roe
Also known as tobiko caviar, the tiny, bright orange, salted eggs of the flying fish have a mild, sweet, fishy flavour. Flying fish roe is used in small amounts as a tasty and decorative garnish for sushi and salads.

fruit tomatoes
Also known as sugar or perfect tomatoes, these small, sweet tomatoes can only be produced under special cultivation conditions which restrict the amount of water they are given. The yield is minimal, but their sugar content is as high as any fruit. Fruit tomatoes are not currently exported to Europe, and have been available in Japan for about 12 years.

gari
Thinly sliced ginger marinated in sweetened rice vinegar is served as a condiment in sushi restaurants so diners can refresh their taste buds between different types of sushi.

garlic shoots
These are the flowering stalks of the garlic plant and look rather like a coarser chive stalk. With a flavour like a cross between garlic and asparagus, they are available from Oriental markets.

ginaan nuts
Better known by their Chinese name gingko, these buff-coloured delicate, sweet nuts are popular in Japanese cooking.

gourd shavings
Known as *kanpyo*, strips or ribbons cut from the flesh of bottle gourds are sold dried. When rehydrated in lukewarm water, they are a popular sushi filling.

hajikami
These pickled shoots of the ginger plant are used to garnish many Japanese meals.

hamo
The complex meaty flavour of conger eel makes it a prized ingredient in Japanese cuisine. Filleting it is one of the great arts of the Japanese kitchen.

ice fish
The odd-looking ghostly Antarctic ice fish is related to the much sought after Chilean sea bass or Patagonian toothfish and has some of its fine distinctive flavour.

ise lobster
This famed spiny lobster with a long beard and bent back is held to bring long life and wisdom. Festivals are held in honour of the delicacy.

ishigaki (giant) clams
The waters around the Japanese island of Ishigaki are famed for their giant clams.

ito-togarashi
Togarashi is the Japanese for 'peppers', and ito means 'thread', thus ito-togarashi are long chillies cut lengthways into long fine threads for use as a garnish.

junsai
Sometimes called 'water shield' in English, this tiny aquatic plant (*Brasenia schreberi*) has long, thread-like stems that grow up from the root. In early summer, the Japanese harvest the water shield's leafy shoots on the surface of ponds and pools. Junsai is sold loose in plastic bags or in bottles.

kaiware daikon
The young shoots of the daikon are used in salads and as a garnish for sushi. Cut off the root ends before using these sharp, spicy shoots.

kalamansi
This small fruit, also know as the sour lime, is small and round with slightly flattened ends. They can be picked green or ripe but the juice stays sour. It is halved and placed alongside dishes of mixed fried noodles and similar one-dish meals, and squeezed over individual servings for a piquant flavour. The juice is used in a cordial concentrate which is diluted to make a refreshing cold drink.

kanpyo
See Gourd shavings.

karashi su-miso
This is a miso mustard vinegar peparation that may be made at home or bought ready-made. You could use the Mustard miso recipe on page 247.

katakuriko
The leaves and flowers of the dogtooth violet (*Erythronium japonicum*) are commonly used as a garnish in Japanese cooking. Flour made from the plant is much prized as a starch and is sometimes used as an expensive alternative to potato flour.

kinki
Known in English as the bighand thornyhead, this large red fish is a species of alfonsino (*Beryx decadactylus*) or bream.

kinoko mushrooms
Literally meaning 'child of a tree', *kinoko* is the word for 'mushroom' in Japanese, but the term tends to be used mostly as a generic for wuild mushrooms.

kinome
Sansho sprigs are called *kinome* in Japanese. These young leaves are used as an edible garnish, chopped herb, or made into a paste. (See Sansho.)

kobe beef
Kobe beef is a special grade of beef from cattle raised in Kobe, Japan. The cattle are massaged with sake and fed a daily diet that includes large amounts of beer. This produces meat that is extraordinarily tender, finely marbled, and full-flavoured. It is also extremely expensive. Because of the high cost and increasing demand, there are now some Kobe-style beef-cattle being raised in the USA, Australia and Scotland using the same techniques; this is often called waygu beef after the breed of cattle used.

kochujang
This is a thick, miso-like fermented chilli bean paste popular in Korean cuisine. Made from soy bean paste, red pepper powder, and glutinous rice flour, it keeps almost indefinitely in the refrigerator. Some brands are hotter than others.

konbu
Konbu (*Laminaria japonica*) is a variety of kelp that grows in the cold seas off the coast of northern Japan, mostly around the northern part of Hokkaido. Rich in monosodium glutamate, konbu is sold in supermarkets as dashi konbu in fairly large pieces for use in making stock. This konbu should never be washed because the flavour lies on the surface. At most, wipe it clean with a cloth and don't leave it in boiling water. Konbu is also a well-known dietary source of iodine and rich in iron. *Shira ita*, or white, konbu is actually pale green kelp, which becomes almost translucent when marinaded.

koyari squid
See Aori squid.

kuzu
Also seen as *kudzu*, this is an Oriental vegetable, the roots of which are generally dried and ground into a powder that is used both as a thickener and as a coating for food being deep-fried.

lotus root
The underwater roots of the lotus water lily may be up to 1.25m long and are generally about 2 5cm in diameter. Peeling their reddish-brown skin reveals creamy-white flesh with a crisp texture and a coconut-like flavour. The roots are available fresh, canned, dried, and candied.

madako octopus
The common octopus (*Octopus vulgarus*) reaches an average size of 60–90cm in length. Called *madako* in Japanese, it can be found throughout the world's warm seas.

maitake mushrooms
This autumn mushroom (*Grifola fondosa*) is fragrant, tasty and very versatile. It is best in a preparation called *maitake no kurumi* in which the mushrooms are dressed with a walnut paste.

makomo-dake
Known in the West as water bamboo or Manchurian wild rice; this plant belongs to the same family as the common bamboo and is closely related to the wild rice of North America. The enlarged stems are harvested, the upper leaves cut off, and only the stem with husk-like wrapper leaves sent to market. The edible portion is the succulent stem after the husks are removed.

mantis shrimp
Actually unrelated to shrimp, these crustaceans are referred to as shrimp because of their front appendages and how they use them to capture food. The description 'mantis' is due to the fact they resemble the appearance and have the same hunting characteristics of a praying mantis insect. Mantis shrimp are popular in Japanese cuisine and often eaten as sushi.

matsutake mushrooms
Of the many kinds of edible mushrooms that grow in Japan, matsutake mushrooms are said to be the king, because of their wonderful aroma and flavour. Matsutake grow in the red pine forests in the autumn, and are a special and very expensive delicacy in Japan at that time.

masago
This is the roe of the smelt fish, which is often used as a sushi topping and garnish.

mirin
This liquid flavouring containing 14% alcohol is used in cooking for its sweetness rather than its alcoholic content. Regular saké cannot be substituted for it.

miru (giant) clams
The Japanese term for the white surf clam. It has a mild, sweet flavour.

miso
This fermented paste of soy beans and either rice or barley with salt is an essential ingredient in the Japanese larder. It is combined with dashi in miso soup and also used as a flavouring for other foods. Red miso, Japan's most popular rice miso, is salty and rich in protein; white miso, on the other hand, is rather sweet. Made from fermented soy beans and barley, moromi miso is never used for making miso soup. This soft, dark brown paste is usually eaten with chilled cucumber.

mizuna
This feathery, delicate salad green (*Brassica campeatris*) is a mildly peppery pot herb that has been cultivated in Japan since antiquity.

molokheiya
This is Egyptian Spinach or melokhai and has a bright green leaf with a soft texture when eaten. In both Mid-Eastern and Asian cultures it is widely used in soups.

momiji-oroshi
This is a preparation consisting of grated daikon mixed with red-hot chilli pepper. It can be bought ready-made or you can make it yourself quite easily by inserting seeds from a chilli into a daikon on the tip of a chopstick and then grating the whole thing.

mongo cuttlefish
The common cuttlefish (*Sepia officinalis*) and the pharaoh cuttlefish (*S. pharaonis*) are both called *mongo ika* in Japanese. The former grows to a maximum length of about 25cm and is familiar in the Mediterranean and east Atlantic. The latter is slightly larger and is prevalent from the Arabian Peninsula across to Japan and Australia.

moromi miso
A type of miso made from fermented barley, but never used for making miso soup. This soft, dark brown paste is most often eaten with chilled cucumber.

myoga ginger
Because only the stems and buds of myoga ginger (*Zingiber mioga*) are eaten, it is hardly recognizable as a type of ginger. It isn't hot like regular ginger and its fragrance is more herbal. The buds are especially aromatic when thinly sliced and used as a garnish.

nigari
Nigari, or bittern, is a concentrated solution of various salts remaining after the crystallization of salt from seawater. The main ingredient should generally be magnesium chloride. Nigari is used as the natural solidifying agent in the preparation of tofu.

nikiri-zake
This sauce for sushi may be bought or made by mixing one part sake to 3-4 parts shoyu (Japanese soy sauce).

nori
Red laver – *asakusa nori* – is harvested and dried in paper-thin sheets of a standard size. The nori is then toasted and used for wrapping sushi rolls, rice balls and futo-maki. Green laver – *aonori* – is harvested, dried and sold in tiny flakes to sprinkle over food. *Aonori* is also an ingredient of shichimi togarashi.

pen shell clams
Also known as fan shell clam or mussel, this is a type of razor clam found embedded in the mud. Once highly popular in Japan, they are now becoming rather rare and highly prized.

ponzu
A citrus-and-soy-sauce dip (see page 248).

red miso
Red miso (*akamiso*) is made from a fermented paste of soy beans and rice. It is red to brown in colour and high in protein and salt.

red vinegar
This sweet and powerful rice vinegar made with saké lees that have been fermented with yeast and the koji mould for three years is the preferred choice of sushi chefs, because relatively little sugar is needed to make the shari-zu for vinegared sushi rice.

rice flour
Japanese rice is of the variety Japonica and is glutinous or sticky. Ground to a flour, it is called *shiratamako* and is used to make sweet mochi dumplings.

rice vinegar
All vinegar produced in Japan is fermented from rice and is mild in flavour, with about 4.2% acidity. Non-rice vinegars cannot be used as substitutes.

rock shrimp
So-called because of their rock-hard shells, rock shrimp are valued for their lobster-like texture and flavour.

rocoto chilli paste
Also known as rocotillo, this relation of the habañero is orange-yellow or deep red when ripe, round with furrows, and tapering to a point. It is mildly fruity and has an intense heat. Essential for ceviches, rocoto chilli paste is available as a commercial product in stores selling ingredients for South American cooking.

sansho
The seedpods of the Japanese pepper (*Zanthoxylum piperitum*) are ground and used as seasoning, especially as one of the seven spices in shichimi togarashi. The sansho is usually sold ground, as it keeps its fragrance quite well. Sansho sprigs (the young leaves are called *kinome* in Japanese) can be used as an edible garnish, chopped herb, or made into a paste.

shakkiri mushrooms
This wild mushroom (*Agrocybe cylindracea*) is found at the foot of willow and maple trees between spring and fall. It has a dark brown cap and grows to a height of between 10 and 15cm. Its flesh is firm and crisp. Marketed as the shakkiri mushroom, nowadays it is cultivated and sold throughout the year.

shichimi togarashi
This 'seven-spice mixture' is a snappy collection of seven dried and ground flavours: red pepper flakes, roughly ground sansho, tiny flakes of mandarin orange peel, black hemp seeds, poppy seeds, tiny flakes of green nori and white sesame seeds. It is available in three strengths – mild, medium and hot – from Asian supermarkets.

shiitake mushrooms
The best-known Japanese mushroom (*Lentinus edodes*) is extensively cultivated and often available in its dried form. Its distinctive pungent flavour goes well with Japanese food. Fresh shiitake are good as tempura, in stews or simply grilled with a little salt.

shimeji mushrooms
This autumn mushroom (*Lycophyllum shimeji*) is known for its excellent flavour rather than its aroma. It has straw-coloured caps about 1cm in diameter. Shimeji come in clumps that grow from a single stem, like miniature oyster mushrooms, at the base of pine trees. Cooking them releases a distinctive flavour and aroma, making them very suitable for soups and other simmered dishes, as well as mixed rice dishes.

shiso
There are both red and green shiso leaves. The red ones (*akajiso*) are mainly used to colour umeboshi and other pickles. The green leaves (*aojiso*) have many uses as a herb, tempura and garnish. Although it is called a perilla or beefsteak plant (*Perilla frutescens*) in English, shiso is actually a member of the mint family. Shiso buds are also used as a condiment, garnish and, when very young, for tempura.

snow crab
This large crab (*Chionoecetes opilio*) is caught in the Sea of Japan in the winter months and served as sashimi, tempura and in vinegared preparations. Snow crab meat is sweet and delicate, with a more fibrous texture than king crab. Its texture ranges from the tender longitudinal fibres of shoulder meat to the firmer fibres of claw meat.

soba
Buckwheat noodles can be eaten either hot or cold. In their simplest form, a dashi-based soup is poured over the boiled noodles for *kake-soba*. When eaten cold, the noodles are served on a bamboo sieve with a dipping sauce. This is called *zaru-soba* (*zaru* being the Japanese for bamboo sieve).

somen
These dried, fine wheat noodles are served cold with a chilled dipping sauce usually in the summer. The noodles are boiled very briefly and then immediately refreshed in cold water.

su-miso
White miso paste thinned with rice vinegar is often used as a dressing.

sudachi
This acidic citrus fruit (*Citrus sudachi*) is a smaller relative of yuzu. It is used in the summer and autumn while still green for its tangy juice and aromatic zest. Sudachi is rarely available outside Japan and lemons can be used as a substitute.

tade
This is the water pepper, smartweed or knotweed plant (*Polygonum hydropiper*). The tiny leaves have a mild peppery flavour and are much used as a garnish for sashimi. The leaves and stems may also be cooked and eaten, and these and the seeds are often made into peppery condiments.

tatami-iwasi (dry-folded sardines)
Sold as sheets and looking a little like thin dried noodles, these are tiny baby sardines that have been quickly pressed and dried. They are used both as a crisp tasty snack and as a flavouring.

tatsoi
A type of white-stemmed pak choy, tatsoi is a very popular green vegetable in Japan. Its very regular and elegant rosette of leaves also make it highly decorative.

tiradito
Tiradito is a South American dish consisting of cut fish and ceviche seasonings. Its name is derived from *tirar* (the Spanish for 'throw') because the fish slices are thrown into the serving bowl.

tomyo pea sprouts
Chinese pea shoots (*dau miui* and *dou miao*) are the handpicked, tender leaves and stems of the snow or garden pea plants, and are used as a light seasoning or added to soups. In Japan, tomyo pea sprouts are cultivated hydroponically and produced throughout the year in bulk. Pea sprouts are more aromatic and delicately flavoured than bean sprouts.

tonka beans
These are the seeds of the large tropical Tonka tree (*Dipteryx odorata*). Their fragrance is reminiscent of newly mown hay and can be used as an adulterant to vanilla. They are said to lighten one's mood and be emotionally balancing.

tonkatsu sauce
Made from vegetables, fruits and spices, this is Japan's version of Worcestershire sauce. Named after the Japanese for pork cutlet, with which it often served, its sweet flavour goes well with fried food.

toro
The belly of tuna is very pale in colour and fatty. Highly prized for sushi and sashimi, it is considered the best cut of the fish.

udo
The white stalks and leaves of this aromatic plant (*Aralia cordata*) are similar to asparagus in taste. The tender young stems can be eaten raw or boiled.

umeboshi
Sour and salty, these are often called Japanese salted plums, but are actually a type of apricot. They are much revered for their reputed health-giving properties.

wakame
This seaweed (*Undaria pinnitifida*) is used in miso soup, salads and other dishes.

wasabi
Although similar in flavour, Japanese horseradish (*Wasabia japonica*) is less harsh and more fragrant than its English cousin. Fresh wasabi is very expensive. It grows wild in cool, shallow pools of pure water, often high in the mountains, and is extensively cultivated under similar conditions. It can also be bought as a powder or paste from Asian supermarkets. *Wasabi zuke*, or pickled wasabi, uses the leaves, flowers, stems and sliced rhizomes.

white miso
White miso (*shiromiso*) is made from a fermented paste of soy beans and rice or barley. It is beige to light brown in colour and quite sweet. A high-grade Kyoto product, white miso is expensive.

yama-imo
This is a white root also known as mountain yam or mountain potato. It is cut into crisp slices as a crunchy accent to roe sushi, or grated and made into a cold porridge.

yama-momo
The Japanese term for the bayberry (*Myrica rubra*).

yariika squid
Yariika or spear squid (*Loligo bleekeri*) is a slender, spear-shaped cephalopod that grows to about 40cm in length. Spear squid are caught in the seas around Japan, particularly in the spring when they come close to the coast to lay their eggs.

yuzu
Japanese citron (*Citrus junos*) is zestier than lemons and not as sweet. Yuzu also has a very potent fragrance. It is used for both its acidic juice and its aromatic rind. Yuzu juice is now available from Asian supermarkets.

yuzu kosho
Available from Japanese markets, this commercial seasoning comprises green chilli, yuzu rind and salt.

Index